Poetry in Motion

Wiltshire
Edited by Claire Tupholme

 Young**Writers**

First published in Great Britain in 2004 by:
Young Writers
Remus House
Coltsfoot Drive
Peterborough
PE2 9JX
Telephone: 01733 890066
Website: www.youngwriters.co.uk

SB ISBN 1 84460 371 7

Foreword

This year, the Young Writers' 'Poetry In Motion' competition proudly presents a showcase of the best poetic talent selected from over 40,000 up-and-coming writers 130.

Young Writers was established in 1991 to promote the reading and writing of poetry within schools and to the youth of today. Our books nurture and inspire confidence in the ability of young writers and provide a snapshot of poems written in schools and at home by budding poets of the future.

The thought effort, imagination and hard work put into each poem impressed us all and the task of selecting poems was a difficult but nevertheless enjoyable experience.

We hope you are as pleased as we are with the final selection and that you and your family continue to be entertained with *Poetry In Motion Wiltshire* for many years to come.

Contents

Marlborough College

Sheldon School

Lauren Cooper (11)	49
Cerys Harry (14)	50
James Parsons (11)	51
Andrew Wright (11)	52
Jack Ibbetson (11)	52
Eloise Molyneaux (11)	53
Deanna Humphries (12)	53
Jessica Mander (15)	54
Josh Blake (11)	55
Bethany Hammond (11)	55
William Tunnicliffe (11)	56
Layli Foroudi (12)	56
Alex Bower (12)	57
Shane Chard (11)	57
Laura Hutchison (11)	58
Christopher Carter (12)	59
Jessica Dabrowski (12)	59
Stephen Farrell (12)	60
Evan Jones (12)	61
Lucy Hart (12)	61
Priya Lanka (12)	62
Vicky Weston (13)	62
Lucy Mead	63
Chloe Nicholas (12)	63
Marta Korycka (11)	64
Jamie Nayar (12)	64
Rose Orchard (12)	65
Valerie Viloria (13)	66
Charlotte Griffiths (14)	67
Becky Woods (12)	68
Toni Easson (12)	69
Hanna Quainton (15)	70
Elina Chin (14)	71
Lucy Aylen (15)	72
Dennis Pike	73
Anne Moore (15)	74
Sam Leadbeater (11)	75
Christopher Walker (15)	76
James Bracey	76
Tim Dutton (11)	77

James Lewis (12)   77
Mark Hulbert   78
John McElhinney (15)   79
Ellis Fawcett (12)   80
Kathryn Boulter (14)   81
Tom Jenkinson (11)   82

The Clarendon School

Sarah Wade (12)	82
Kerena Sheath (11)	83
Claire Louise Davies (11)	83
Jenny Egar (11)	84
Daniel Pearson (11)	85
Charlotte Robbins (12)	85
Ruth Bailey (12)	86
Andrew Sheppard (11)	86
Carly Stone (13)	87
Sophia Smith (11)	87
Angela Bunce (13)	88
Rachel Kay (11)	88
Sadie-Louise Geen (11)	89
Katie Baker (11)	89
Isabel Lucas (11)	90
Nik Williams (12)	90
Angela Wyatt (11)	91
Emma Hurren (11)	91
Rachel Clare (12)	92
Samantha Knight (11)	92
Hannah Derrick (12)	93
Rianna Rose Lilly Ball (11)	93
Hayley Naylor (11)	94
Paul Rush (11)	94
Paul Ireland (11)	95
Rebecca Lanfear (11)	95
Leah Coombs (11)	96
Kimberley Jane Gee (11)	96
Naomi Henry (13)	97
Robyn Hartley (12)	97
Rebekah Edwards (12)	98
Laura Price (11)	99
Stacey Hadley (11)	100

Rebecca Coles (12)   100
Kerry Hopper (12)   101
Aaron Osman (12)   101
Jack Muir (12)   102
Hannah Greenman (12)   103
Emma Griffin-Banable (12)   104
Ashley Cradock (11)   104
Kristy Dyson (11)   105
Tom Bartlett (11)   106
Gary Dell (11)   106
Kirsty Adams (12)   107
Ryan Spong (11)   107
Louise Allberry (12)   108
Kelly Ellis (11)   108
Naomi Lowson (11)   109
Hannah Phillips (11)   109
Matthew McLaughlin (12)   110

The Cotswold Community School
Douglas Rose (13)   110
Daniel Blackmore (15)   111
Jake Simmonds (12)   111
Joshua Robinson (12)   112
Cameron Picton (14)   112

Westwood St Thomas CE School
April Walker   113
Tasha Glew (15)   114
Suzi Milne   115

Wootton Bassett School
Daniel Robinson (12)   115
Mark Lazenby (15)   116
James Rowell (15)   117
Katherine Wilson (11)   118
Lauren Ratcliffe (11)   118
Hannah Day (11)   119
Daniel Jupe (11)   119
Allanah Skuse (11)   120
Edward Sanger (12)   120

Liam Rowe (13)   146
Tom Doherty (11)   146
Kathryn Dixon (14)   147
Amber Brown (11)   147
James Sexton (11)   148
Amy Aitken (11)   148
Maddie Humphries (12)   149
Sophie Warlow (12)   150
Sam Davies (11)   151

The Poems

Untitled

Importance I try to run
I try to hide
But you're always there.
Right by my side
And so I decide
To turn to you
And suddenly
I don't know what to do
You speak to me with no words
How can this be?
It's so absurd
We share a smile and swap a glance
Without you I'd wither like plants
But now it's time to say goodbye
I can't be with you and this is why
Your screaming and screeching
I could not stand
Your kicking and slapping
Got out of hand
It went too far
You got too deadly
Your threats came true
Your hand was steady
Your hand plunged down
Knife gripped tight
It ripped into me
And I followed the white light
It wasn't your fault
The fits came hard
And now it's too late
I played my last card
And do not worry
I forgive you
Live on without me
Do what you have to
I sit up here
From this cloud here
And look at you
I see you flounder
I wonder how
Your fits were cured
When my life ended
Were you then secured?

Sebastian Bird (15)

King Of The Waters

Teeth sharp as daggers
Scales like a suit of armour,
King of the waters.
He slid down the river bank like a toboggan down a hill
The water around him shimmered like diamonds.
All that showed of him was the evergreen scales on his back
And his piercing eyes yellow like the sun.
His eyes turned to face the side, fast as lightning
And he dived under, just as quick.
There on the other side of the river bank stood his prey.
He popped his head out of the water
Graceful as a ballerina he leapt out of the water and seized his prey.
He sank his razor-sharp teeth into his victim
And, like a tornado, spun frantically . . . silence . . .
Suddenly, like a dolphin he jumped out of the water and spun
Landing in the water and reappearing at the other end.
Dinner is served.

Lydia Reeder (11)
Greendown Community School

The Cockatoo

With his eyes like minute, black marbles
He scans across the deep, dark blackness of the night.
With his wings as white as a crescent moon
He readies to fly and glides through the night sky.
The wind pushes him back with powerful arms
But he is stronger.
His night-black beak lets out a squawk
His stick-like legs and curve-bladed talons
Grasp and perch onto a wooden branch
A sudden squawk startles him
A small, white snowy owl flies towards him
And like a thunderbolt
He falls . . .

Mike Porter (11)
Greendown Community School

How To Eat A Physalis

First whiff the fragrance
And let the scent fill your nose
Note: you feel like you're on
A tropical island.

Perceive the cabbage-like fruit
With a tomato inside
Manipulate the crispy case
And the squidgy, sticky stuffing.

Coil the crunchy leaves
And tear them off
Count to three . . . 1 . . . 2 . . . 3
Take a deep breath.

Slowly take the ultimate bite;
Juices wildly running
Sweet, sour then fruity
Now you're in paradise.

Helen Rogers (11)
Greendown Community School

Football

Football is great, football is good,
it gets me through my childhood.

Football is cool, football is great,
it is my best mate.

Football is super, football is cool,
it can easily stand tall.

In the end footie is cool
so if you wanna be a star
keep on kicking that ball!

Joseph Kerley (12)
Greendown Community School

Kiwi Poem

Just observe the pea-green fruit,
Let the sight take over.
Then slice, let the juices run
Pick up and feel the sliminess.

Smell the uncertain, bitter fragrance
And let your taste buds burst with excitement,
Gently place inside your watering mouth,
Taste the sourness and quiver.

Finally - crush,
Juices flow into teeth and gum,
Your taste buds are going wild
Swallow
it speeds down your throat like a water slide.

At last it flows into your welcoming stomach,
Your brain wants more
You start to lick your lips,
As you slice another one.

Darryl Carpenter (11)
Greendown Community School

The Circus

The clowns laugh and joke all day,
On the tightrope where they sway,
The lion tamer's lions look fierce,
It's like a lion's growl piercing
The clowns juggle under and over
It's as if he's got good luck
From a clover!

Catherine Forty (11)
Greendown Community School

The Wolves Of The Night

The moon appears and the echo of voices begins,
One by one the wolves appear with the serenade of the moon's song.
Looking up at the sky the wolves are entranced,
And then they begin to howl,
'Moo-oo-oon,' they cry as they stare at the beauty
And with this they recite the ancient moon song,
'Oh moon, oh moon, how beautiful you are
Oh moon, oh moon, how did you get there with the stars?
If only I were up there with you
Oh if only I could see all around
And understand the way the world goes . . .
Oh moon, if only . . . '
And with this line they go down to the lake
And drink the water which has trapped the moon's soul,
As they drink they watch the moon glide through the water
And as the moon reaches the edge of the lake the wolves return home
And retire to the warm confines of slumber.

Daniel Mountain (11)
Greendown Community School

Easter

Easter has come,
Let's joke and be funny,
I hope I get Easter eggs,
From the Easter bunny!

Over there in the pot,
No! There's nothing there!
Over there by the chair,
Yes, I've found a lot!

Now it's the end,
Of all the fun,
I can't wait till next year,
Until all the fun has begun!

Alicia Atherton (11)
Greendown Community School

Dolphins

Graceful, calm creature,
Swims all day,
Grasshopper when he jumps to the clouds,
Slowly glides catching fish,
Gobbles them up and looks for more,
He sometimes sings,
But not for long,
Sounds like a squeaky mouse,
One day he sees a fish,
He can't resist,
he was the predator,
Or was he?
The angel of death pounced on him,
Net choked his neck,
He struggled out,
The lucky one,
But many are not so fortunate.

Laura Hammersley (11)
Greendown Community School

Megan My Rabbit

My rabbit is called Megan
And she's nine years old.
I got her when she was only two
And now she's crooked and old.

Her eyes twinkle like two bright stars
That dazzle in the night,
She's a little teddy bear
She's friendly and won't bite.

I love my rabbit Megan
I've had her for so long
Now the problem I must face
Is soon she will be gone.

Hannah Webb (11)
Greendown Community School

How To Eat A Banana

Touch its smooth skin,
over the bumpy layer underneath
dig your nails into the skin,
peel your fruit;

Excitedly run your fingers over the rough skin
as it rises up to your watering mouth,
it opens in welcome.

Pop the fruit into the black hole
feel it wash soothingly around your mouth,
its strong scent and taste,
find they're being crushed.

A delicious, fruity fragrance
seeps out, swallow,
slide it wildly down the frightening slide,
know you can recapitulate.

Jenny Snook (11)
Greendown Community School

Winter

Winter is a beast
Bitter and cold
An evil creature
From a story told and told.
Birds come in summer
But winter banishes them
It's as secretive as a cat
And as precious as a gem.
But when winter gets tired
There's something else waiting
Just around the corner
He's warm, refreshing and even invigorating
He will banish winter again
For another year
But winter will be back and what will happen then?

Thomas Jackson (13)
Greendown Community School

The Cat

Like Heaven, its cosy bed softens it as she sleeps.
Stirring suddenly from a deep sleep,
The cat disturbed and intrigued by a clatter outside,
Wanders slowly into the kitchen.

She cries at the door and gently paws it.
She scuttles outside into the warm, hot sun of the garden,
She prowls the area like a hunter and sees movement in the hedges,
Unsettled, she creeps closer and pointed for movement, she stops.

The guest realises it's unwelcome and runs as quick as a flash,
With pride and happiness she starts to groom herself.
Her tongue combing her ruffled coat,
But with flames of anger in her eyes she constantly stares into the
                                        luscious green grass.

Feeling no need to stay out any longer,
She sneaks back inside to continue her afternoon siesta.

Catherine Pinner (11)
Greendown Community School

The Old Man

There was an old man
He lived in my town
When he grew up
He grew down.

He lived in my street
But he had big feet
When he would walk
He would never talk.

He was like a dwarf
With a wobbling head
But now he's dead.

Amardeep Singh Chana (12)
Greendown Community School

The Hopping Adventure

She lies motionless in the hot summer heat.
Slowly she moves to munch on a carrot.
Then she rustles about in her soft bed of hay.
Her ears prick,
Footsteps.
Warm arms wrap around her,
Voices, about her ears, as soft as silk they say.
After a short cuddle she gets placed in the long grass.
As she is hopping freely, it feels like the flowers are hopping with her.
Her eyes are sparkling stars.
Suddenly,
She stops and has a good scratch and clean.
She senses hands coming closer,
So she starts hopping, faster, faster,
Till the hands catch her.
She has been defeated,
Back into her hutch, awaiting her next adventure.

Jessica Price (11)
Greendown Community School

Christmas Joy

Christmas has come
I'm really excited
I've been good all year
So Santa's delighted.

Christmas is the time
For all the fun
The decorations are up
And now it's begun.

It's Christmas Eve now
I can't get to sleep
I can't wait for Santa to come
So I can have a peep.

Sophie Workman (11)
Greendown Community School

Haunted House

As he walked through the door
And looked at the floor
He said, 'What a strange place this is.'

He looked at the ceiling
And got that strange feeling
Where you feel as if you're being watched.

He walked up the stairs
Although unaware
Of the evil following him.

When he reached the top
He turned and stopped
And opened the bedroom door.

He sat on the bed
And raised his head
To see the beast stalking him.

He jumped to his feet
And pulled off the sheet
In which he trapped the beast.

He ran out the door
And fell through the floor
Into the basement below.

He found a long sword
And looked through the board
From which he fell through.

The beast had jumped down
And was rushing around
So he impaled it on his sword.

He left the house
As quiet as a mouse
And was never heard from again.

Callum Walker Stirton (11)
Greendown Community School

The Sea Lion

His emerald eyes open wide
His whiskers stand up on end
He groans to the other sea lions
This drives them round the bend.

He jumps into the sea
Like a bouncy diver
His tummy rumbles
And he dribbles out saliva.

A big fat fish swims by
The big tiger pounces
And catches his prey
'Look at my fish,' he announces.

A net comes down
But he doesn't see
Darkness is above him
He's now in Heaven, not the sea.

Jessie Howard (11)
Greendown Community School

The Lost Girl

She sits there lying on the desert floor,
Waiting for someone to come.
Sitting there so quietly, patiently
Oh waiting, waiting in the scorching hot weather,
Stumbling, falling over,
She gets up
So lonely she walks,
With her footsteps sinking in the sand,
Wishing/hoping there's someone to play,
Unfortunately she died,
The poor thing,
All she did was wander
Day and night.

Nicola Rooke (11)
Greendown Community School

The Tortoise

In the sweltering heat, he plods steadily onwards
His black eyes glittering in the sun.
All around him a soft breeze tickles the grass,
Whispering into the sunlit air, urging him forward.

His black and brown shell feels as heavy as the world,
But he holds his head aloft,
He is a soldier, determined to reach his goal,
He is getting closer.

A smile plays around his mouth as he comes to the water's edge,
He has reached it,
The river lies there silently,
Waiting for him,
He lowers his head and drinks.

His thirst quenched,
He turns around and starts the journey home,
In the sweltering heat, he plods steadily onwards,
His black eyes glittering in the sun.

Judith Ruddle (11)
Greendown Community School

Haunted Ship

She sits upright in her chair,
She thinks someone is around,
The waves splash up at the ship as if it is attacking it
A shadow walks past the window
'Who was that?' she whispers to herself
She gets up from her chair and opens the door,
'Boo!' goes her son
And that was the end for that woman.

Daniel Gentleman (12)
Greendown Community School

Attack Of The Living Torpedoes

Blurs, zooming through the water,
Like stealth torpedoes they strike their lunar target,
Their streamlined bodies scatter the clan
As they devour their fishy feast,
Their powerful shots overwhelm their prey as long jaws snap them up,
They spot their aerial nemesis,
Like bombs they drop to the seabed
The cannons are ready to fire,
They build up power,
Confidence sky-rockets,
Cannons blast forth the living missiles,
Then the others pounce and swallow the target,
Mission accomplished!

Mathew Willis (11)
Greendown Community School

The Leopard

She's as blotchy as a Dalmatian
And as her whiskers spike out
She defends her baby whilst speaking to it.

She listens for movement
And she hears something
Her mouth opens wide
As rapid as a motorbike.

She's angry
When she's angry
She's a volcano
Waiting to erupt
She leaps, tries to kill.

Danielle Woods (11)
Greendown Community School

Feisty Feline

Stretches ginger-striped body,
Back arches like a rainbow,
Back to normal in a flash,
Tip-tap of the tins reaches delicate ears.

Open and aware,
Tiny movement catches glaring eye,
Stares leopard-like searching for prey,
Protecting like new mother.

Seeks where premises lie,
Wraps around like long-lost love,
Awaiting affection
Hunger equal to starving lion.

Hunger eased,
Sprawls in the sun like an overfed holidaymaker,
Purr soothes
Like breeze rustling through trees.

Naomi Coombs (11)
Greendown Community School

Hiding

Hide under a hurdle,
Struggle to stay fresh,
With short, tubby necks,
They examine the silky, cool sheet,
Surrounding them,
They sway side to side,
As they journey through
A crusty, pale-coated surface,
Their long, black flippers
Are as gloomy as a moonless night.

Steven Sharpe (11)
Greendown Community School

The Tiger Cub

This tiger cub lived on the prairie,
His fur was spotty and furry,
He ran like the wind,
He could disappear like a ghost.

They come to hunt him,
Trees and bushes all around,
Protection from the bad men
He stays in his pack.

Mother tiger always there,
Looking out for her babies,
They see a chance to escape,
They are the wind,
He is a plane taking off.

Jamie Baker (11)
Greendown Community School

The Shadow

Sitting, raring to go,
Feet like lily pads
He hears the sound
Races off
Bouncing in his step
His ears are rubber tree leaves
Flapping in the wind.
His body a compact parcel
Cloaked in paper, the colour of a silver moon
The athlete returns from his feast full and tired
Stretching his legs like an elastic band
He curls up and rests.

Siân Gannon (11)
Greendown Community School

The Beautiful Dolphin

Families wait anxiously!
Children sit quietly!
While a beautiful, young dolphin swims beneath the water.

He looks around to see what he can see,
Nothing is to be seen!
But light blue, clear water.

He has soft, smooth skin like a baby's bottom
He's a small dolphin,
But a wise dolphin.

He swims just below the top of the surface
Suddenly, he comes out of the water
And flies high into the air
He flips over like a gymnast.

The audience cheer in amazement
And he swims back down into the clear water.

Polly-Marie Hemmings (11)
Greendown Community School

The Purr-fect Cat

Standing like orange gem stones,
Long, tall and charming,
Round like a spiky twig,
Sharp, pointy ears,
Eyes, shutting doors,
Strong and unique,
Ready to lie down in the later summer sun,
The cat, sleeping at peace,
Before the hunting begins,
The purr-fect animal with a human likeness,
Looking for its dinner.

Victoria Rogers (11)
Greendown Community School

How To Eat A Pineapple

Feel your way around
the suspect in question
spikes spurting from nowhere
but in every direction.

Smell its scented aroma
just like a petal of a rose
it's delicate
as I smell and touch.

Get a knife and cut
from head to toe.

I open my mouth
slowly - put it in
I bite, then swallow
now it's gone
take another one.

Zoe Archer (11)
Greendown Community School

My Rabbit

The fair brown fur on her back is as soft as velvet,
Her sharp black eyes shimmer in the night.

She leans against the garden fence looking into the sky,
Whilst she's eating her apple crunchies
I come outside and stroke her on her soft back.

She yawns and you can see her sharp white teeth shining,
Her claws are like knives as she scrapes the sawdust to make her bed,
My rabbit is the best.

Leigh Foster (11)
Greendown Community School

How To Eat A Pineapple

Place hands on rough, uneven skin,
Take note of the spiky leaves,
Tropical colours reminding you of exotic palms.

Take knife,
Lay pineapple on its side,
Plunge blade through rough skin.

Next take a deep breath in,
Smell sunny, tropical juices,
Carry on with the cutting,
Scalp the pineapple.

Put a slice through your lips and into your mouth,
Feel bumpy flesh with your tongue,
Let sweet juices fill your mouth.

Crush and chew the slice
And within a minute the first slice has gone.

Emily Bissex (11)
Greendown Community School

Juicy Pineapple

First feel rocky skin,
Then hands on soft green leaves
And the white base as hard as steel.

You sniff once and again,
While the saliva floods your mouth,
You slice the skin off,
While you lick your lips.

You take your first bite,
You're in Heaven,
Your teeth dig into it
And swallow.

Stephen Bowell (11)
Greendown Community School

A Cute Canadian Lynx

Hiding away in a hole of a tree,
Waiting for his prey.

His dark eyes like a black sky are fixed on the ground,
Looking for any sudden movements.

Suddenly he hears a leaf rustle,
He leaps out of the tree stretching himself to the limit.

Landing silently he approaches his prey,
All you can hear is something like a
Gust of soft wind as the lynx breathes.

He pounces on the leaf, it seems he was startled
For nothing but a bug.
So the lynx retreats, his eyes are mad with fury.

He climbs back into the tree to wait silently again.

Katie Brigginshaw (11)
Greendown Community School

Archie

Tuft of hair falls over his ears,
A whinny of delight
And a small smile.

Honest eyes covered with fluttering eyelashes,
Deep-set chest lined with broad shoulders
Like a layer of chocolate his coat runs over his muscled body.

White socks stamp
Shaking his glossy mane
Not resisting the temptation
He bucks with joy
Hooves clatter everywhere.

With a cheeky smile
Laying down
Archie rolls around in horsy bliss!

Sadie Northway (12)
Greendown Community School

How To Eat A Kiwi

First stroke the hairy kiwi
Next pick it up,
Roll the precious fruit
In your hand.

Observe the round kiwi
Take in every last detail
Of the luscious fruit
And memorise forever.

Then pick up the round fruit
And smell the fruit
Of summer goodness
That will always be there.

After, take a tiny bite
And take a huge bite,
Crush the fruit with your big molars
And finally swallow the sweet taste.

Hear the fruit
Scream for help,
As it squelches through your mouth,
Down into the deep, dark stomach pit.

Thomas Morland (11)
Greendown Community School

Mouse

Minute and small
Crawling
Twitching his tiny, wet nose
As he nibbles through food with razor-sharp teeth
While watching for enemies
Intelligent, flashing eyes dart
Surveying every inch of ground
Climbing every step one by one
Always watching!

Daniel Rodgers (11)
Greendown Community School

The Pig And The Wolf

The pig trots along
Lazily trudging
After a scrumptious meal.

Now in the shining sun
He falls asleep, dreaming about food.

There is something - a predator.
His sensitive, pointy ears could hear a pin drop
His snout-like nose could smell dinner, if it was in another country.
But the only thing he can smell is danger.

Now he sees a flash
The predator's a wolf
The wolf attacks
The pig dances out the way
Then fights back with tusks and trotters.

The wolf retreats
Never to come back
He is as scared as a whimpering mouse
The pig, snuffling, goes back to sleep.

Michael Campbell (12)
Greendown Community School

Stingrays

As he swims swiftly through the sea,
With his eyes wide open like beads,
Walking in the soft, stony sand,
He spotted something moving in the distance, coming quick
Jumping in the sand as quick as a flash, hiding in the sand.

He jumps out to catch his prey
Swinging its sting-like tail killing it.
And eats it up and leaves its bones.

Brown and white spotted back
Shining like diamonds.

James Lederman (11)
Greendown Community School

Innocence

Cute, cuddly with a little button nose,
  Rabbit and dog described.
For the innocence in their little brown eyes
  And the happiness in their faces.
Asleep at night, but at daytime they play in the garden
  They run around content as can be, they are free.

Round the gushing fish pond, running, speeding through the grass,
The wind whipping through their little faces as if taming a lion,
On their way to the dense undergrowth of the plum tree.

Then they walk lazily inside for the time has come for night,
And as they lay, their eyes slowly droop until they are asleep!

Chloe Barnes (11)
Greendown Community School

How To Eat A Grape

First feel the smooth skin,
soft like a pillow.

Next smell the hint of wine.

Spy on the green oval as it
rolls in your hand.

Taste the tender, juicy grape
as you chomp it in your
mouth endlessly.
Observing every little bit
of the sweetness.

Hear the squelching
noise as you eat it.

When you finish,
eat another one!

Bernadette Florendo (11)
Greendown Community School

How To Eat A Grape

First touch the smooth, green skin
And spy on the wondrous fruit.
Inhale the sweet, normal smell
Of the great wonderful figure.

Observe the glorious, tender taste,
One half is gone.
Nibble a bit more of the tender,
Green, squelchy delight.

As you keep nibbling the juice
Oozes and screams, your face lights up
You love this taste.

The grape has been nearly eaten
Your happiness swells as the last
Bite of the delight has gone
The grape is dead.

Laura Dunham (11)
Greendown Community School

How To Eat An Orange

First, smell
Then touch the ruffled skin,
Feel the taste in your mouth,
Now smell the orange whiff.

Now the tension is getting nearer,
You start to feel water dripping out of your mouth
And thinking more of that yummy
Orange!

As you start peeling,
The smell is getting nearer,
Then the first slice is a dream come true.

Finally, the tangy orange has gone.

Holly Callan (11)
Greendown Community School

Polar Bear

The mighty beast lies lazily under the sun.
Looking around he slowly clambers upon all fours.
He smells the cold, damp air with his wet nose.
He smells a gun!
He gathers his white, fluffy family
They hide in the shimmering, shining snow
As quiet as mice.
The wind whispers in his ear
A shiver climbs up his back.

He does not smell the danger anymore . . .
Slowly he stands up.
Bang!
He falls.

Vicki Hotson (11)
Greendown Community School

How To Eat A Kiwi

First hold the fruit and take a quick niff.
Then take a deep breath.
Examine the fresh, brown fruit.
Let its short, rough, hairy skin irritate your palm!

Dissect your juicy kiwi into eighths.
Observe the seeds drowned by a jelly-like substance.

Swiftly hide your front fangs inside the green jelly,
Rip the substance from its cotton, hairy-like skin.
Drain the rich liquid.

Finally, swallow the small remnants from your drooling mouth!

Harry Townsend (11)
Greendown Community School

The Frog

Brightly coloured as a flame
Too poisonous to touch
Its pointed head and giant black eyes aware of every move
Skin as slimy as a slug allowing it to breathe.

It sits still
Sees something
Frozen to the spot
Eyes focused
Suddenly its tongue shoots out wrapping round the prey
He winds it in like a fishing rod and gobbles up his meal.

Then he does a springy leap and bounces away like a spacehopper
Plunging in water, he swims a fast breaststroke
Pedal feet power him
Surfacing to breathe he burps a loud, joyful croak
He dives down
Disappears.

Flip Holtrop (11)
Greendown Community School

Kitten

As silent as a mouse,
He delicately tiptoes around,
Miaowing gently as he walks,
His skin of fur as soft as a teddy bear,
Black and white.
A tiny nose peeping out,
He searches for milk,
Then he hears a noise.
Suddenly he scampers behind the sofa,
Danger's over
He slowly opens his mouth
And a silent yawn comes out,
As he softly lies down to
Relax.

Danae Watson (11)
Greendown Community School

The Mischievous Cat

She stares right through the camera
Her black and white tail wags from side to side.
Her dinner awaits!
She has been caught by the camera
Trying to catch her food.
Her tummy rumbles like rough sea
Splashing against the rocks.
Her two ears point like two church steeples.
Licking her lips, her whiskers twitch
She is eyeing up her prey.
She considers her next move to catch it.
When the camera is looking away,
The victim darts to the glassy wall
Trying to escape from the plate.
Hiding behind a plant.
Now the camera is packed away
Her tail starts to waggle again.
She smiles!

Hayley Jefferies (11)
Greendown Community School

The Lost Mates

As blue as the Caribbean oceans,
She glides through the salty sea,
Making shrill whistles to her lost mates
With no reply she swims to the surface.

Playfully she jumps out of the water like a child at a birthday party
Confidently her curved, triangular fins rise
And become a ship's sail pushing away the air.
Scanning the water she spots them,
Spinning, twirling, splashing back into the ocean.

Her tail becomes a gymnast's foot hovering in the air.
Reunited they swim to the depths like ghosts at sunrise.
Playing, jumping, leaping,
Never lost again.

Sadie Tuttle (11)
Greendown Community School

The Fox

As he stumbles onto a log,
The mother cheers him on.

His growling bark startles
Other small creatures.

His light flame fur,
Surrounds the cute eyes.

Arrowpoint's steam
Captures the angry mouth.

Beady, black nose,
And trowel ears
Make him not at all like a dog.

Black, bushy tail
Burnt charcoal feet.

The young month-old creature,
Who lives under a shed, pounces
And he catches, his mother by his side.

Jonathan Rabbitt (11)
Greendown Community School

The Raven's Claws

Sharp as a knife, sharp as a sword
Swooping down with its jagged claws.
Its prey runs end on end
Didn't see what was round the bed.
It was the claws of doom
Looking for its prey so soon.
The raven's claws are dangerous
Step in the way and your life is at an end.

Lewis Coombs (11)
Greendown Community School

How To Eat A Pineapple

First sniff -
and let taste buds go wild;
note sourness
round mouth and tongue.

Observe juices; don't let drip,
then nibble: Braille promises
through fingertip and thumb
of tastes to come.

Next bite;
sink into its
golden bumpy flesh
chew slowly.

Close lips;
gasp, roll the prize
through dark, red core
with tongue.

Now - crush!
Squeeze, listen, pause
let juice and pulp invade
with summer sourness . . .

Until - *boom!* It's all gone
Now take another slice.

Stephen Jones (11)
Greendown Community School

Elephant

A boulder rolling over dry, cracked land,
Like the folds of the Earth he is lined by time,
Baggy, wrinkled skin a landscape, a map;
Ancient eyes sigh.
Meant to protect, his bent, white swords now endanger.
Cobwebbed eyelashes hide innocent,
Wide old eyes from the beating sun,
His antennae, another eye, brushes between leaves as
It searches and forages, snuffles and twitches,
Snacking on forest giants.
Focused and aware, he lumbers over the sun-baked earth,
Fan ears flapping.
A distant gunshot startles him.
Panicked, the moving mountain on tree-trunk legs
Dances in slow motion.
His warning bellow, a trumpet foghorn, threatens to stampede -
Earth-shaking, earthquaking,
Trampling tangled undergrowth beneath spiny, pebbled pads,
Broad barges floating now over squelchy mud
He plods into the warm, brown river,
Swooshing giant tidal waves,
To sink in relieved, cooled.
Playfully he dives his trunk and sprays a joyous fountain,
Sapphire, crystal, gold.

Mrs Urquhart's Year 7 Group
Greendown Community School

My Cat

Large, emerald eyes rest upon a relaxed face,
Light purrs fill the room,
Complete comfort is expressed
As she stretches and yawns in a dream.

A sudden squeak alerts her,
A quiet voice from behind.

Now sprung upon her stick legs,
Binocular eyes search and scan the empty room.

Swiftly and silently,
She creeps into the garden,
Ears pricked at the slightest sound.

Heart beating wildly, she lets out yelps of excitement
And with one swish of her snake-like tail,
She leaps into the bush.

Triumphantly,
She struts across the lawn,
Rodent clutched in her powerful jaws.

Standing on two feet,
She scratches and scrapes at the door,
Waiting for me . . .

Daisy Leahy (11)
Greendown Community School

So What!

She sits there
She is alone
Nobody likes her
So what if she's different?
So what if they're the same?
She finds it hard
Nobody knows her pain.

She'll dig a hole
Deep in her soul
Find a way
But won't make them pay
What are her thoughts?
What is her pain?
I will not cry
I won't let them kill me
They may laugh because I'm different
But I laugh because they're all the same.

Emily Collett (13)
Greendown Community School

Autumn

The warm sun fades and a new chill stirs,
Autumn in her stealthy, insidious way
Has approached, dancing through the changing years
A bitter cold creeps into the fresh day.

It shocks the blithe swallows and awakens whispering breezes,
The pale flowers die and crisp golden leaves
Flutter gently to the hardening ground as it freezes,
Groans and sighs are amongst the bare, stripped trees.

Summer is sweetly forgotten as it moves to September,
Deep orange, russet red and other colours fill the air,
Green foliage and covered branches will not be remembered,
Short days return fast as nature mourns in despair.

Charlotte Duncan (14)
Marlborough College

Soft Wretch

As I lie in my bed, the lights and distractions of the day gone.
I am left to fight with the now familiar pain
That lingers in the crag of my soul by day,
By night, wriggles uninvited to the surface.
My eyes give up the battle to stay dry
And I turn, on a damp pillow of empty tears,
Waiting endlessly for sleep to visit.

A love story I barely speak of tangles itself inside me.
I curse the cruel wish I naively made,
For a life of heightened emotions,
As I spend a psychological moment,
Which turns to a cold, neglecting stare.
Eyes fixed on absence while hands shake
Then clutch tight, hating helplessness.

I curl up small, envelop myself in a wild fixity.
A sound rudely awakens my senses.
It withdraws me from my heavy solitude.
Dignity grabs a hold, only to let go fast,
Letting my eyes fill with troubled tears,
Mind struggle with amorphous thoughts.
A desolate heart groans in the dark.

Desperate, I panic, trying to shake off this spell.
It forces forward subconscious thoughts.
I meditate - calm - soft,
Whatever. Screw the effort.
Insomnia creates more time for thought.
Time is dangerous for my lyrical psyche
It will spin out of control; steal my sanity.

What emotion would be most in - keeping with my true nature?
Love? Glory? Ambition?
What fits my dramatic temperament?

My eyelids become leaden, interrupted sleep draws near.
Some rest for the solitary wretch.
When the sun rises on a new day,
I swear to breathe a new breath.
As if freeing myself from a hot desert,
To inhale clean, fresh mountain air,
Which will heal the painful wounds.

Something that has become so luminously destructive
in the depth of my soul, I refuse to call *love*.

Clare Newcome (17)
Marlborough College

From Place To Place

A whispering wood
A horn blows
The silence shattered
A hurricane of crashing hooves

Nearby a sleeping village
Embedded in time
Thoughts of days gone by
A life that still lives

Onto the bustling city
Endless hurry and frenzy
Forever against time
No place for peace

The great gull swoops down
Over pounding, crashing waves
Hurled onto weathered, white cliffs
Wind swirling with salt

A prism of difference
Stretched under clouded sky
Shapes changing
History everlasting.

Kimberley Botwright (14)
Marlborough College

Britain

There's a place in Britain special to me,
Beyond the peninsular, far out to sea . . .

Palm trees disturbed by the frenzied breeze,
Cause shrieking gulls to rise from the trees.

Tropical flowers are lush and bright,
What I like is the silence of night.
The starry sky sparkles above,
But tranquillity is what I love.

The long, white beaches are littered with jewels,
Hidden treasures, shells in rock pools.
The perfect white sand is eaten by sea,
Whilst pompous seals surface and gaze at me.

Behind the headland the waves crash and roar,
- Giants stampeding, destroying the shore.
Ragged rocks resist the attack,
Desperately holding the angry waves back.

To contrast with the ocean's azure blue,
Is heathland, cloaked in imperial hue.

In storms the ferry, regal and great,
Small dancing dinghies bow in its wake.

Lapped by the gulf, secluded and warm,
Tresco is different from the British norm.

Matilda Kay (14)
Marlborough College

The Four Seasons Of Hampstead Heath

Rolling hills of open fields
Next to huge gangs of trees
Overlooking the landscape
Watching it as time changes

In winter the smells of old, decaying wood take over
The sound of cold rivers gush down mossy rocks
The shades of brown
Make the woods one of luxury

In spring animals crawl out from their comas
Buds grow on trees
Filling the woods with life and energy
Bringing colour back while birds chirp and rabbits hop

Summer lakes hidden in bands of trees
Are lightened up by streams of life
Emitting their beauty
While flowers blossom, making the woods
A place of joy

In autumn the woods are a place of wonder
People lie on the carpets of leaves
Orange, yellow and brown
Thinking silently
But still the woods are full of spirit and life
Before winter consumes the woods

The woods have survived many years surrounded
Surrounded by the dirty, noisy roads of London
Refusing to fall to the dark world of modern buildings
But still shedding its everlasting magnificence
To us!

Nick Horowitz (14)
Marlborough College

Ra! Ra! England

Memories of England tend to be mostly about rain,
Barbou and wellies, hunting and champagne
The wonders of toasting crumpets,
When outside, 'Oh look more rain!'
Then reaching for a marshmallow as if it's *such* a pain.

In winter, all the mud sitting there as if to say
Come jump, squish, squelch in me
As if it's going the next day.

England seems to be about horses,
It's like the south's nearly obsessed
But it's really Daddy's way of proving
That his little girl's clearly the best.
So when it comes to pony club,
And Mummy's seriously overdressed
Daddy'll pay, wink and nudge
To make sure Lucinda and Snowy beat the rest.

At first glance England seems to revolve round
Rugby and prep schools,
But if you look closer,
You'll see there are a set of rules.
These are rules one must try to follow
If one is trying hard to please
The most snobbish and uppercrust
Of British societies.

Number one, be fashionably late
Let's say 10 minutes at the least
Number two make sure your favourite film
Is 'Notting Hill' or 'Beauty and the Beast'
Number three if you're a girl
Is drink whisky and play Black Jack
For these are qualities you'll need
If you want an invite back.

Number five if you're a bloke
is always hold open doors
because all British women
can and will find out your flaws.
Number six might sound silly
but could be most important of all,
is always be able to tell the difference
between a cricket and croquet ball!

Alexandra Bailey (13)
Marlborough College

Sheep

In the desolate country of Wales,
Where the rain beats down and the wind gales,
A sheep sits huddled all alone,
Wondering where to make his home.
He decided to make for a nearby wood,
Where many great, tall evergreens stood,
He crept right out from under his shelter
And danced down the hill helter-skelter.
The rain kept pouring down and down,
The mud splashed up and his coat turned brown.
When he reached the edge of the wood,
He rushed inside as quick as he could,
Under the shelter it was all so dry
And it was all so dark - you couldn't see a fly.
He was suddenly overcome by sleep,
Something rather uncommon for sheep,
So he lay right down up against a willow
And used its trunk as an uncomfortable pillow.

Justin Scarfe
Marlborough College

Smell

I do recall, somewhere in my mind's eye
That smell
Oh that smell
A day of baked beans and cheese
Surely was responsible for the
Unnatural action
Room dark
Silence
Bang! As small explosion
Distinguishes itself amongst
That eerie silence
That starry night sky
Became dark and misty
That smell
Oh that smell
Imagine, just imagine
That smell
Oh that smell
I press my nose to
The windowpane
In hope of finding some
Kindly god to whisk me
Away.
Nothing
Hands burn
For a door, a momentary
Gasp of fresh air
That smell
Oh that smell
At the door
Cramming their bodies
Into the dark room
They came flocking
In numbers to
Witness
That smell
Oh that smell

Were they interested?
Were they curious?
But why? Why go and
Sample what people are
Dying leave?
That smell
Oh that smell
Door passes
Safe again
Air, fresh air
May the kingdom of
God be praised
That smell
Oh that smell
After twenty minutes
The crowd dispersed
Curiosity, interest
Vanished
Darkness
Converged into
Light
Smell
What smell?

Tom Durant-Pritchard (16)
Marlborough College

A Winter's Day

The church bells sing across the open moor
The frozen rushes tingle in the breeze.
Steam rises up from the mouths of children
Running back and forth on the virgin snow.
Laughter can be heard from a mile away;
From the children throwing snowballs in the fields.
The sun glistens on the bright white carpet,
Stretching out across its winding path
Of snowflakes sparkling like diamonds.
Far off over the golden horizon,
Smoke rises from the bellowing chimneys
Like a leaf caught in a current of air.
Gently rising higher and higher
Rocking to and fro in the soft wind.
Floating slowly towards the setting sun
It glows warmly with a tint of orange.
The sun draws gradually closer
To the still beckoning horizon.
The twilight sky draws ever truer,
Casting a permanent shadow over the plain.

Lucy Gordon (14)
Marlborough College

Pok Fulam

Seeing a pimpernel in the undergrowth,
leaves small and rounded,
petals dark and scarlet-red,
nothing disturbs him from his life,
he smiles in the sun and laughs in the wind.

Yet, at night-time if you enter
the forest, the air cools,
the wolves howl to each other,
talking about their day,
the wind whistles through the trees,
rain comes and goes.

Pok Fulam was a beautiful place
near was the volcano Popocatepetl,
erupting every so often,
schmucks think that it is extinct
until they experience the rumble,
soon it will come again, again,
soon it will come.

Thick, slowly moving
down the mountain,
people screaming and running quick,
just not fast enough for this speed,
people homeless, people dead,
families sad for their loss,
he grins with success,
killing a hundred or two,
nobody knows what to do,
but still people live near,
but still, but still.

Anna Gordon (13)
Marlborough College

Britain

An Englishman without his dog,
Is something rather rare,
In muddy ditch and master's bed,
They are quite the inseparable pair.

With gun on shoulder and dog at heel
They stride about the land
Tweed jackets with pockets and wellington boots
And a lead clasped in one hand.

A shoot lunch is a fine affair
With a roast, some wine and a fire
Then they all set out in their four-wheel drives
With many a muddy tyre.

The birds soar into the azure sky
Guns rattle a random beat
The pheasants which fall are retrieved by the dogs
And brought to their masters' feet.

Loyal to each other, retiring together
Both gentlemen to the end,
It has to be said that a dog truly is
A man's most faithful best friend.

Verity Macdonald (14)
Marlborough College

Animals' Names

Animals come in many different shapes,
Fish like the wrasse,
Mammals like the lynx
They also have different names.

These range from adder to zebra
Names can sound odd,
Or be spelt weirdly,
Puma and panda are examples.

The speed of a salmon,
The colours of a sturgeon,
The skill of a squirrel
And the spring of a springbok.

The two odd bods of the group
Are the platypus and the echidna
Both are egg-laying mammals,
One characteristic not meant for them.

All animals are alike,
One way or another,
So I would say, that
Chipmunk is my brother.

Andrew Cumine (13)
Marlborough College

Bewildering Names

The beautiful resonance of the didgeridoo,
The plummeting putridness of tiramasu.

Popocatopetl found in Mexico,
A Celt's tam-o'-shanter with his kilt far from low.

Taramasalata and aubergine,
Their pitiful hues stretching only to green.

The Chinese prefer the ravishing Shanghai,
Where specific rules only apply.

Trash can, garbage, jello too,
The French resort to 'petit filous'.

Northerners would relish a plate of chips,
Gravy engulfing every fragment of their lips.

Although a rather pompous man,
Would have no idea about Saskatchewan.

A mere concoction of avocado and kedgeree,
An intellectual would resist and rather be free.

Will Perkins (13)
Marlborough College

Words I Love The Most

I love the way words work my mind,
From the oozing of Jacuzzi,
To the short and blunt blue chit.
Gliding smoothly as if silk I like the word ylang-ylang
But not so much as Twiglet.

I adore the swishing of Shanghai
And the weird and wonderful Timbuktu,
The drawling tone of Alabama,
To the madness of Bombay.
I love them all just the same
In every single way.

The butchness of the Mexican
To the queerness of a Celt
These are words with no excitement
To the wonderfulness of Gaelic.

All these words I love the same
Even if they sound a bit lame.

Rory Cramsie (13)
Marlborough College

Why Such Names?

Names of things can be awfully funny,
Like a simple rabbit, when young is a bunny,
A chip is a food, a churchman a monk,
But a chipmunk when combined to form one.

A kangaroo or didgeridoo,
A swimming pool, black; Blackpool,
A sweet little penguin, a scurrying squirrel,
Manta ray in the sea, or Napoleon Wrasse.

Ho Chi Minh city or the castle that is new,
Pumpernickel, pomegranate, pompous, papaya,
Why is eggplant aubergine or zucchini courgette?
Why so many new places? New York, New Jersey?

Singh, a common name among Sikhs,
But also the act of sweet-voiced people,
Animals like chameleon and platypus,
An Australian animal, koala,
Add Lumpur and it's an Asian city.

You can scuba-dive in the Maldives,
Or take a place, Chester,
Turn that place into a man
And the product is Manchester.

Patrick von Behr (13)
Marlborough College

Hong Kong Names

In Hong Kong the names you find might be funny,
But over there, they're as normal as a bunny.
The prime minister being Tung Chee-Wa,
It's more exotic than Tony Blair.

The food is delicious and very well known,
It's been making its business all on its own.
Dim Sum, Peking duck, Hoi Sin sauce and black beans,
Sweet and sour and noodles are completely unseen.

Those aren't the only odd names in store,
The islands around there, are almost as before.
There is Lantau and Lamma, Chek Lap Kok and Pok Fui,
Sai Kung, Kowloon, Pok Fu Lam and Ko Toi.

On a junk for the weekend you may escape,
From Tai Tam or Wan Chai this journey you will make.
There are wonderfully tongue-twisting words you may find,
But now back to Marlborough, leave Hong Kong behind.

Emily Botsford (13)
Marlborough College

England

Britain; an island
An island filled with endless towns and villages
The rare city.

London for example
A maze
A jungle of complications.
Roads. Left, right, left, right
Up
Down
Down
Underground, over ground - you choose.

Endless buildings soar higher and higher
Like tall, towering trees terrorising you.

People, too many people
Every second of the day - white, black, mixed.
Standing, waiting, talking.

Hoot, *shout*, screech, natter
Noise never goes away
Never rests
Never leaves
Noise you could drown in.

Roads left, right, up, down,
Buildings soaring up, up, up
Too many people
Hoot, *shout*, screech, natter.

A lost child's worst nightmare
He turns left - busy road
He turns right - towering trees
He shouts - one in many
He looks - too many people.
Lost in London
Nightmare!

Aimee Taberer (15)
Marlborough College

England

Rolling hills and a shimmering sea,
There is no other place I'd rather be.
Golden beaches like a gilted edge,
Which surround the shamrock emerald ledge.

Above the beaches you hear the seagulls cry,
While the fluffy, white clouds drift gracefully by.
Fish jumping here and there,
In and out of the warm summer's air.

Hills and valleys all lush and green,
With so many secrets waiting to be seen.
Winding streams, rippling pools
And woodland forests in which are animals big and small.

There are patchwork fields of ochre and gold,
With rambling bushes and trees that are old.
Hopping rabbits and fluttering birds,
These are some of the mysteries untold.

Antonia Chope (13)
Marlborough College

The Things I'd Miss Most

If I were to go away for a day
These are the things I'd miss . . .
The beautiful birds singing sweetly early in the morning,
Food freshly cooked for me
My baby sister babbling away all day
The sweet smell of my mum's flowers
The delicate sound of the clock ticking at night
My garden's fresh air after lots of rain
My cosy, warm bed
The light smell of my mum's steam from her iron
And the soft smell of my clothes after they've been washed
These are the things I would miss most.

Lauren Cooper (11)
Sheldon School

A Crying Place

A crying place
Once where my father lived

A crying place
When a sudden heart attack took place
No chance to express our spoken words,
Not even a chance to kiss and hug farewell
No warning
Not even a sign.

A crying place
From four to two
From happy and bustling
To silence and grief.

Pain and loneliness took over our home
Crying
Grieving, forever broken
Hearts in a crying place.

I devised a plan and volunteered
To help our community collect their trash.
I did it from day to day
For my mother's sake
So I could grieve without her feeling pain.

I hid in shadows of dark bushes
Crying until no tears would come
Then returned to my house
To sleep for the next bereaving day to come.

One evening when it came for chores
I collected the trash and sat alone
In the shadows of the bushes
Where a misty sky above me
Where no light came upon me.

When I returned to the crying place
My mother sat alone in the darkened basement
Weeping herself out.
She hid her pain, like I hid mine
To protect me from hurting.

The pain I suffer openly,
The pain I suffer alone.
I'm not sure which is greater
Or which one really hurts.

Like the stab of a knife
Or the shot of a gun
I don't know which is greater.

We held each other,
Poured our hearts out
Then realised . . .
We never needed to cry alone again
In the crying place.

Cerys Harry (14)
Sheldon School

The Things I Would Miss!

Splashing water sounds so nice
Having hot chocolate while feeling like ice
Watching fish swim all day long
Listening to my favourite song
The smell of fresh bread makes me smile
Making chocolate last a while
I love to feel my cat's warm fur
I also love to hear him purr.

Sweet lavender brightens my day
Home time, 'Oh yeah!'
I love the feel of my guitar
I also love my dad's cool car
The taste of sweets so sour
Playing on the computer for an hour
Spaghetti getting cooked smells great
Climbing rough trees with a mate
These are all my favourite things
That I would greatly miss!

James Parsons (11)
Sheldon School

Things I'd Miss

If I had to go away forever, the things I would miss are . . .
The sight of my mum and dad,
The sound of rain beating on the window,
The taste of ice cream,
The feeling of a soft, fluffy bear
And the smell of flowers,
The sight of fireworks exploding,
Listening to people speaking,
The taste of an ice-cold fizzy drink,
Touching my cat's fluffy fur,
The smell of freshly picked berries,
The sight of newly-grown flowers,
Listening to calm music,
The taste of a burger.
The feeling of silk running through my fingers,
The smell of a clean quilt,
The sound of birds singing,
The feeling of being cold.
These are the things I would miss.

Andrew Wright (11)
Sheldon School

Summer

When summer is here,
You go out and play,
You have so much fun,
Till the sun goes away,
You play with your friends,
You get up to mischief,
You play in the garden,
You play in the street.

Jack Ibbetson (11)
Sheldon School

The Things I Love Are . . .

The things I love are . . .
When I'm at the shops and I see sweets;
My cat's soft, warm fur,
Hot, crunchy toast in the morning
And the cars at night when I sleep.
The smell of smoke that comes from a candle,
Presents at Christmas and my birthday,
The soft touch of my Beanies,
Ice cream on a hot summer's day.
The soft pitter-patter of raindrops on my window,
The smell of freshly baked bread,
The sight of my baby cousin playing,
The way I sink into my mattress while I sleep,
The taste of apple juice,
The sound of the television,
The cold smell of mossy air at night,
It is all of these I will miss.

Eloise Molyneaux (11)
Sheldon School

When I Was Young

When I was young I wrote on the walls,
And never got told off,
But now I would get grounded,
Oh, joy of being young!

I used to put my prints everywhere
And never got told off.
But now I would have to clean everything,
Oh, joy of being young!

I also miss my free time with Mum,
I have no time anymore.
She used to tuck me in at night,
Now, that's what I truly miss!

Deanna Humphries (12)
Sheldon School

Him

He was born into this world
To do great things
He was beaten down

Down
Down
Down

To the depth of nothingness,
He regained control and survived.
His creator was snatched away from him

He didn't survive

The man that was brought into this world
Did great things
As I watch him hunched over
Surviving

Save him

Gentle, unpoisoned tears rolling down his face.
Black flowers blossom
Feel the life evolving

Do you feel like someone?

Waves dash him
Fire burns him
Life kills him

Faith will begin and you will be
Entwined in a cocoon of love

He weeps, until he has no weeping left
Lying at the bottom of all things
Utterly worn out
Utterly pure.

Jessica Mander (15)
Sheldon School

Sad I Ams

I am . . .
The pigsty with the rotten trough,
The dolphin with a really bad cough.

I am . . .
The dishcloth that's tattered and torn,
The T-shirt that's never been worn.

I am . . .
The ink pen that's always had a leak,
The mountain with no peak.

I am . . .
The tree that fell on the floor,
The house that has not got a single door.

I am nobody,
Nobody special.

Josh Blake (11)
Sheldon School

My Favourite Memories

These are the things I'd miss . . .
Soft, smooth, sensitive silk passing the skin on my body
The sight of a clear blue sky
Crunchy chicken dippers
The sweet smell of rose and cinnamon
Church bells swinging to and fro
A marble floor, glistening in the sun
Tomato soup running down my throat
The fragrance of fresh coffee in the morning
The pleased purr of a tabby cat sitting on the fence
The flickering flame of a candle
Cool and creamy cottage cheese
Those are the things I'd miss.

Bethany Hammond (11)
Sheldon School

Feelings

Revenge!
Revenge is sweet!
Revenge hurts!
Revenge is like being stabbed!
It is like a gunshot!

Jealousy!
Jealousy is harsh!
It is like being bullied!
It hurts to even think about it!
It burns the back of your brain!

Love!
Love is like a soft breeze!
It smells like strawberry ice cream!
It tastes like melted chocolate!
Love is romantic!

William Tunnicliffe (11)
Sheldon School

Winter

It will snow
The wind will blow
The winter will come
The summer is done.

Must keep warm
With scarves, hats and gloves
The summer is done
The winter will come.

Layli Foroudi (12)
Sheldon School

Dance Class

Toes tapping,
1, 2, 3,
Hands clapping rhythmically.

Legs kicking way up high,
Arms waving in the sky.

Pirouetting across the floor,
Spinning, spinning
More and more.

Bodies stretched high and wide,
Ballet shoes tightly tied.

Skirts flowing round and round,
Feet prancing along the ground.

Flying, leaping through the air,
Dancing, dancing without a care.

Alex Bower (12)
Sheldon School

What A Woman!

A woman is not critical,
But more than just a miracle.

Her baby-blue eyes
Never tell lies,
For she is more beautiful
Than the setting sun.

Her long golden hair
Is much more than fair,
She really will care
For you anywhere.

And her heart full of love
Sparkles like an innocent dove.

Shane Chard (11)
Sheldon School

The Hunt

Hear the clatter of hooves
Thundering on the floor.
Dust in your eyes
Yet the breeze is cool.

Hear the trumpet,
Blown by man.
His merciless laugh
I run as fast as I can.

There's no escape,
All exits are blocked,
It's all I can take,
As I clatter to the floor.

My last gasp of breath,
As I fall to the ground.
The hounds tear my life and limbs away,
I wait to be found,

To be dragged away,
As proof of the kill
But at least I am dead
And not running still.

Laura Hutchison (11)
Sheldon School

The Moods Of The Sea

Rough with power and might,
Happening either day or night.
Crashing against the rocks,
Surrounding the exposed docks.

Calm and peaceful it can be,
Setting all your worries free.
Tranquil waves, sunny beams,
Stopping the arguing and the screams.

Oysters' pearls,
Mermaids' curls
Sharks and their dangerous teeth,
Fish, seaweed and the coral reef.

Moods of the sea can change from day to day,
If you don't watch your guard you'll have to pay!
Without the sea,
Where would we be?

Christopher Carter (12)
Sheldon School

Snowman

Snowman, snowman standing there
In the cold night's winter air.

You stand there in the freezing cold,
Tall, white, still and bold.

The sun rises up, dawn breaks
Like the ice on the lakes.

A new blanket covers the ground
Because of the snowballs round, round, round.

The frozen icicles on the trees
Like the sting of the bees.

Children go in, as the sun goes down
Goodbye snowman in the town.

Jessica Dabrowski (12)
Sheldon School

Golly, Golly, Golly

Golly, golly, golly,
I'm off to France on my jolly,
It's gonna be fun,
In the red-hot sun
Golly, golly, golly.

Hurray, hurray, hurray,
Today is the day,
We're going away,
And we're off to play,
Hurray, hurray, hurray.

Cool, cool, cool,
I'm off to play in the pool,
While the sun beats down,
I'll swim around,
Cool, cool, cool.

Ouch, ouch, ouch,
The sun has caught me out,
My skin's real sore,
I had to withdraw,
Ouch, ouch, ouch.

Pack, pack, pack,
Everything into a sack,
It's just gone three,
It's time for my tea,
Pack, pack, pack.

Goodbye, goodbye, goodbye,
We're about to go and fly,
I'll be home soon,
Around about noon,
Goodbye, goodbye, goodbye.

Stephen Farrell (12)
Sheldon School

My Sister

I have a little sister
She likes to kick and bite.
She jumps on me at 3am
And gives me such a fright.

And when she was very young,
She kept us up at night.
And when she had a tantrum,
It really was a sight!

I woke up in the morning,
And I really don't know how.
But she had led into my room,
A massive Jersey cow!

But the really bad thing is,
It's actually getting worse -
In exactly sixty seconds,
She'll take over this verse!
Unswiaock!

Evan Jones (12)
Sheldon School

Red

Red roses
Poppies too
Valentine hearts
For a lover of you
Hot as the sun high in the sky
All of these red
I wonder why?
Red!

Lucy Hart (12)
Sheldon School

The Cat's Story

I am a stray,
I live far away.
Fishing through the rubbish bin,
Finding empty tuna tins.

But what's here before me,
A mouse do I see
For I must be dreaming,
I'll catch the mouse for tea.

Hungrily, I am watching it,
But it does not look back.
Watching it with cunning eyes,
Suddenly I attack.

I pounced on it and pinned it down,
And ripped it with all my might.
I started eating, chewing, swallowing,
And there was not a drop of blood in sight.

Priya Lanka (12)
Sheldon School

In The Sky!

The clouds float,
The birds fly.
I wonder what it would be like
In the sky.

Everything's so peaceful,
Nothing to disturb it.
Everything is graceful,
In the sky.

Why does it change,
Day to night?
Fading shadows,
In the sky.

Vicky Weston (13)
Sheldon School

Teenagers

We love to chat
We love to cry
And we're really not
That shy!

We're irritating
Time wasting
And we truthfully
Never lie!

We try to be good
But always fail
If we don't get our way
We start to wail

We're moody, stressy
And awfully messy
But we honestly don't
Know why!

Lucy Mead
Sheldon School

A Very Special Mum

My mum is amazing,
So loving and warm
She's guided me safely
Away from each storm.
She's a shoulder to cry on
When life is unkind
With a mixture of wisdom
And humour combined.
Whenever I'm near her
I always feel glad
Because my mum is the best friend
That I've ever had.

Chloe Nicholas (12)
Sheldon School

Things I'd Miss

The sweet scent of roses in the garden,
The crackling of burning wood at night
With the royal, rich flames blaring high up with delight;
The softness and warmth of babies' skin;
These are the things I would miss.

Delicious chocolate melting in my mouth,
Smiles of friends that I see every day,
And teachers saying, 'Have a great holiday!'
These are the things I would miss.

The smell of coffee and my dad's barbecue
Chicken and crusty homemade bread;
These are the things I would miss.

Teachers saying hello to you at the start of the day,
My grans waving to me as we come to stay.
Sleek, silky ribbon, fluttering in the air;
And also the feel of my dog's fluffy, black fur.

Marta Korycka (11)
Sheldon School

Dragons

Dragons, dragons flying higher,
Dragons, dragons breathing fire.

Hatching out of little eggs,
Growing wings and little legs.

Their teeth are a bloody mess
From biting through the rancid flesh.

They swoop down from above,
Their wings outstretched like a dove.

No trace of blood left behind,
The bodies they will never find.

'There's no such thing,' you might say,
But you'll be sorry when you're the prey.

Jamie Nayar (12)
Sheldon School

Nearly A Teenager

I'm nearly a teenager
But feel like a child
I'm in adolescence
Growing up is so wild.

My hormones are racing,
They start then they stop
It's a bit like a roller coaster
You swoop then you drop.

I have some bad hair days
And bad moods to boot
Then there are great days
When life is a hoot

The zits are quite awful
They cause such a stir
But at least they're not catching
My friends all concur.

Best mates are essential
They know how you feel
When I get temperamental
They don't make a big deal

I wish it was over and
I was fully grown up
It'll happen some day
'Til then I'll shut up!

Rose Orchard (12)
Sheldon School

I Wish I Had A Nu Fone

I lyk fones,
I tlk on them 24/7
If I get free tym,
It's lyk b-ing in Heaven.

I dnt lyk my fone now,
I wish I had a nu 1.
My fone has bad 'n' boring games,
And it's taking out all the fun.

I always get junkmail,
It's really annoying.
If I try 'n' fone bak
Then I have 2 keep holding.

If u think I'm bad,
Then look @ my cousins.
They always tlk on the fone,
As if it costs nothing.

Wen I get a nu fone,
I'll play wiv it all the tym.
If sum1 tries 2 get it,
I'll shout 1000 tyms, *'It's mine!'*

I no it sounds lyk I hav no lyf,
But I dnt really care.
Coz 1 day wen I go home,
It will b sitting under the Xmas tree there.

Valerie Viloria (13)
Sheldon School

Primary School

Into the classrooms that creak underfoot,
Then searching for your friends amongst the crowd,
Delicious shades of sugar paper stuck to the walls,
The clatter of chairs as seats are chosen,
Winter draws near, the days get dark,
And rain splashes the windows.

Puddles grow and smother the playground,
A world of gloom is taking over
Damp hair pushed back out of frozen faces,
Excitement fills the air like a whisper . . . Christmas,
Tacky decorations pinned to the walls,
Glitter spills off the handmade Christmas cards.

A new world of growth inside and out,
The impatient child longing to be free,
Yellow shining daffodils reflect the sun, and glisten,
The work plasters the room with bold pictures,
A medal of honour worn with the greatest pride.

The sun floods the school with light,
A field of blue and white striped dresses,
Stickers on work marked and correct,
Everything smaller than before,
Stupid games fade and conversations emerge,
The end of term at the tips of their fingers.

The wall-faded sweetness is peeled away,
A bare room characterless and empty,
Work piled high as mountains,
A time line of names from squiggles to scribbles,
Reports cause the mountains to tumble,
Sending a year's work to the floor.

Charlotte Griffiths (14)
Sheldon School

Winter Is Coming

Winter is coming and it's getting cold,
It's a time where new things start to unfold,
It's snowing now, every drop is pure white,
We are in the snow having a snowball fight.

I want to build a snowman,
And stop it from melting, if I can,
I'm with all my friends and we're having fun,
It's really cold and no sign of the sun.

There is no grass to be seen,
Not even a patch of green,
Lots of animals are hidden away,
No sign of any wildlife all through the day.

All the trees are bare,
I'm wearing a hat that covers my hair,
I have a coat to keep me warm,
There's frost everywhere, on the front lawn.

It's getting too cold to stay outside,
It looks like I'll have to go inside,
It's teatime now, and I'm really tired,
I'm lying on the couch in front of the fire.

I'm nice and warm now and I'm in bed,
I'm all snuggled up, resting my head,
It was great fun today, like a rabbit in its burrow,
But now I have to sleep, and the fun will come back again tomorrow.

Becky Woods (12)
Sheldon School

The Bad Box

I have a secret box and in that secret box
I keep the things I hate
I can't bear *men*
Cheering
Roaring as they watch football
I wish I could stop it
Now I can.

I hate the fact that people
Don't share their love
Killing
Beating your children
It's selfish
Stop it now!
I wish I could stop it
Now I can!

I despise rain
Maybe lots of sun

With just a bit of breeze
I wish I could stop it
Now I can
I'll make sure this box stays safe
Under my bed
Just in case
Maybe one day
I'll want that *bad thing* back.

Toni Easson (12)
Sheldon School

Pandora's Box

It haunts me every day
In every waking, breathing way
I don't know what I'm supposed to say
I'm not good at advice
I'm not good at emotional sacrifice
You will never know how I truly feel
My feelings are fake, they aren't real
If I let them flood like you do
I would be too much like you
I'm not ready to let out the person I am inside
Maybe if I did, I'd feel more alive
Is it sad to watch somebody die?
Is it etiquette to instantly cry?
How can people deal with the pain -
Of never seeing them again?
It just faded after a while
Like the fated wood to the eternal file
It has died, it's not what it was
Days go by and time does pass
I'm locked up in this Pandora's box
Chained and barred, trapped and locked
Somebody please let me out
Nobody ever hears my shouts
I scream, I twist inside myself
I need someone to come and help
Somebody please let me out
I don't have breath left to shout.

Hanna Quainton (15)
Sheldon School

Cabbages

I looked at the raw, black Earth which I had just tilled,
And stretched forth my arm, to let the seeds spill;
They fell, like beads of rain,
With the speed of a slow, ongoing freight train;
I covered them up with the fresh-smelling soil,
And I waited, waited and waited!
I patiently waited for the reward to my toil.
The months passed by, showing no signs at all, nothing!
My mother watched me, complaining and tutting,
Then something small and green sprang out,
I laughed at my mother, the old trout!
For I had grown something whilst she just sat, lazy,
To me, the world was spinning and going hazy.
The cabbages sprang!
Oh how they shooted!
They unfurled with the buds of flowers.
But then my mother strode forth
Armed with a small shovel and a basket -
I watched her in fear and wished that I could lock my beautiful
Cabbages into a casket.
She dug them up, showing no mercy,
Singing her fearsome war song.
She took them inside to the kitchen and speared one with
A long, sharp tong.
'My sweet, they are ready to eat and you have grown our lovely meal.
How proud you must be to grow us some food which is worth
More than a pea!'
She cackled like a witch.
She laughed and ended up with a stitch.
And my beautiful cabbages?
They are gone, gone, gone!

Elina Chin (14)
Sheldon School

Mrs Webb's Class

Whether you played 'tag', 'hopscotch' or 'grandmother's footsteps',
screams of excitement always ended in tears.
Pair after pair of holey tights tossed in the bin.
Then the screech of a whistle and it was nursery rhymes around
Mrs Webb's chair.
Your fumbling fingers fiddled with the threads of the carpet,
as you stared up at her in wonder.
As you worked, you could sniff out a recently sharpened pencil,
taste the tang of Mrs Webb's perfume; savour the taste of
leather shoes
All this, as you laugh at the face beaming up at you from
your rewarded portrait.

You could make it into a competition for who had the brightest
lunch box!
And then a catastrophe, you can't open your chocolate bar.
Your eyes sting with tears and Mrs Webb, the super heroine,
rushes to your aid.
She would titter away at anything, even your latest wobbly tooth.

It was Christmas and the classroom glittered like a treasure trove,
gold, sapphire, rubies, emeralds.
Swirls, whirls, stars and shimmering lights.
Best of all was Mrs Webb's rosy-red smile.
She was our queen of the classroom; her tinselled chair was
a magical throne.
Her long cardigans were her royal robes,
Her hairband was her diamond crown.

And then the chairs begin to shrink,
A sudden anger grows and you kick your friend for copying you.
You're sent to the quiet room in disgrace!
Instead of the playground, it's the field.
It's time for daisy chain making with your friends again,
clustered around in your den.
Usually you give your daisy chain to Mrs Webb, but you're
flustered and selfish and angry again.

Suddenly, you're bursting to know about everything in the world.
You confide in your queen and she chortles and brushes you away.
And suddenly it dawns on you; you're just another annoying child
in the way!

Lucy Aylen (15)
Sheldon School

Things I Love

I love the rush of a red cricket ball hurtling
towards me;
I love the sound of an engine revving up.
I love the taste of home cooked meals.
I love it all.
I love the touch of cold, soft snow,
I love the smell of roses in the garden.
I love the sight of my dinner coming in.
I love it all.
I love hearing the end of school bell,
I love my cereal in the morning.
I love silk, it's so smooth.
I love it all.
I love the smell of petrol,
I love my music beating.
I love a full-cooked breakfast.
I love it all.
I love to stroke my dog;
I love the smell of food being cooked.
I love to see all my friends and family -
I love life!

Dennis Pike
Sheldon School

Primary School

We sat cross-legged on the coarse, camel-haired carpet,
Staring at the purple painted toenails of the teacher
And her voice drifted down from far away.
A melody which held us in awe.

And what a clutter of things to learn,
So special, like the thousand paper snowflakes which
We made at break, when the rain lashed down,
And the jungle-hot, humid classroom, simmered with smells.
A whole new world to conquer.

Then when the sun peeped out again at lunch
We'd tumble into the whirling tempest of the playground,
With shy, smiling, friendly faces, fun and games.

The older ones were fierce beasts, charging at motor boat speed,
Leaving you in the wake of their tidal wave,
Tears flowing, ripped trousers, cut knees.
Suddenly again you'd be swooped upon and cuddled
At the teacher's side.
The sweet scent of her flowery perfume and special attention
                                                    healing all.

Later you'd grimace and display your cuts with a grim warrior-like pride
Sitting in the plastic city of the lunch canteen, reflected in mirror mazes
Of pink Barbie lunch boxes.
Hearing the clashing crescendos of an orchestra of shrieks,
Amongst the wafting odour of fried fats.

At home, you were still half there. Amongst the fluorescent
                                                    neon displays,
With the stapler click, click, clicking like a woodpecker,
And your pencils scritch-scratching. Your brow folded in concentration.
To have your work put up was the equivalent of an Olympic
                                                    gold medal.

Best of all was sharpening your pencil, the grated chocolate,
                                                    swirly curls,
The fresh wood smell mingled with lead and the roughness
Against your fingers.
Then without realising, the pencil had shrunk down to nothing.

And as all those sharpenings fell to the floor, time was ticking away,
Summer's melting past and before you knew it,
You were the big fish in a small, little pond.
You were so huge, you could look down on the pineapple top
Of the teacher's ponytail.

There was nothing more to discover now,
Primary school was a discarded, faded toy.
Shrunk behind your miniature desks, captured inside a prison
                                                    of routine,
You stared wistfully beyond the classroom and longed for freedom.

Anne Moore (15)
Sheldon School

The Things I'd Miss

The things I'd miss if I wasn't here are -
The smell of freshly cut grass,
The taste of a divinely cooked Sunday roast.
The laughter of my baby cousins,
The love of my mum and dad.

I would miss the enjoyment of wrestling with my brother,
The feel of Christmas presents being opened under the tree.
The excitement of playing on the PlayStation,
The laughter of playing with my friends,
The comfort of lying on my bed or beanbag.

I would miss the feel of melted chocolate,
The enjoyment of practising on my skateboard.
The feel of kicking a football around;
The sound of bouncing a basketball.
The excitement of swimming in a gala.

I would miss the feel of stroking animals' fur,
The taste of sweets going into my stomach.
The excitement of building and playing Warhammer;
The taste of my parents' food.
The enjoyment of going on holiday.

Sam Leadbeater (11)
Sheldon School

The Primary Cloak Of The Young

Summer-scented blades disperse around a hasty foot,
The latest obsession is the plague of fickle youth.
You stand with the dark presence of the superior,
Deeply contrasted with the blue dome of inspiration.

Eager students gaze in awe at bright luscious shades,
Thin, smooth pages, chessboards with large squares.
A pleasant, familiar odour infiltrates the day's scent,
Luring your attention to a powder-tainted blackboard.

Your teacher wields words of antiquated origin,
Her hand poised around 'The Ghost of Thomas Kempe'.
Ensnared with a quaint urge to create,
An untrained hand corrupts a carefully directed trail of ink.

Your once desperate hunger becomes a memory,
As you acknowledge solid green and white trees.
Pools of brown over your dinner,
And yellow over your sweet are more solid than liquid.

The air becomes hard and dense with anticipation,
The very sound of the bell becomes tangible.
You leave the ground not looking back at rusted gates,
The past becomes insignificant in the new challenges ahead.

Christopher Walker (15)
Sheldon School

Sea Poem

The sea is like a lion breathing,
Blowing water out of its mouth
Like a rocket shooting into the sky.
His claws are like metal chalk,
Scraping against a wall with sparks
(Water smashing against heavy rocks).
The tidal wave is like its mouth
Bites big into a deer's heavy stomach.

James Bracey
Sheldon School

My Favourite Things

The sight of ice-cold snow,
The calming sound of chirping birds,
The sweet taste of sugar, fizzing in my mouth.
The fruity taste of juicy apples,
These are the things I like.

The fresh smell of newly washed clothes,
The grumbling sound of a muddy tractor,
The feeling of a soft blanket.
The warm sight of my colourful bedroom,
These are the things I like.

The musical sound of my CDs
The wonderful taste of chocolate melting in my mouth,
The jolly smell of cut grass,
The softness of my hamster's fur.
These are the things I like.

Tim Dutton   (11)
Sheldon School

My Poem

The clarinet is very loud
It can be very quiet,
It's also good in classical,
In jazz it's just a riot.

The piano is called the pianoforte
That means it's quiet and loud.
It has two pedals called damper pedals,
And makes an eager crowd.

The guitar needs strumming to work,
It has six long strings,
There are lots of different chords to play,
Like A, B and C.

James Lewis   (12)
Sheldon School

Reception

You'd walk in eager to start again,
Lunchbox in one hand reading book in the other,
You take your block, dinner or packed lunch?
With the register done, you start to have a fun lesson,
Water and sand, you would use them all
The messier it was, the better it would be.
As break time was announced, young smiles would greet the
Teacher as you filed out for a break.

The fresh smell of ginger biscuits would greet your nose,
One of the most anticipated things of the day
Nose tickled with flavour, tastebuds tingling,
You dribbled onto the field in clumps.

You would stand and stare in awe;
An older child would be standing high in the air,
Standing atop the climbing frame he would jump . . .
Suspended in the air, your eyes would be fixed,
In what seemed like an age, he would hit the bark carpet,
A splash would arise and you would be showered in bark.

So many things you would have to say,
You would babble on for an age at the simple question:
How was school today then?

Mark Hulbert
Sheldon School

School Memories

On that sunny September morning
Feared children trudge down shadowy corridors.
The dominating buildings strike a sense of dread into the timid.
After several emotional moments, your parents depart
Leaving you in the presence of the superior.

Your early schooldays are a blur to you now,
However certain events are as vivid as ever.
The striking of a bell signals the start of the day,
Your own personal tray brings a glow to your face
As too does a sticker which the teacher presses to your chest.
You wear it with pride.

Lunchtime was a different experience,
The anticipation of what your mother has packed you was chilling.
Lunchtime saw the break up of friendships
But also the renewal of others.
Despite the cuts and grazes obtained,
Lunchtime was a joyous occasion.

As you creep into July, the summer holidays are approaching,
The children all hold a feeling of contained excitement.
When the final day arrives you say your goodbyes
And as the bell is rung for the final time, you break into a run
And continue to run until you break through your front door.

John McElhinney (15)
Sheldon School

The Bad Box

On my desk in my room is a box. It's medium-sized,
pink and fluffy but is awful because there are the things
which I really hate in it.

Some things I hate can be really silly, like spiders,
all black and hairy, but some can be long-legged and thin.
I hate them so much.
Go away and stay away!

However, not all things I hate are silly,
In fact some are pretty serious
For instance, *war!*
I hate it! And it happens everywhere.
It happens in classrooms and between countries.
Stop it! Stop it now!

One personal thing I really despise is
People touching and lolling all over me.
I just hate it. I don't know why? I just do!
I also hate it when people fiddle with my hair.
Stop it. Stop it now!

This box of mine will stay there,
It will stay there, locked forever.
Until one day it won't be able
To hold them.
They will follow me forever.

Ellis Fawcett (12)
Sheldon School

Untitled

Reading figures and numbers,
Our tiny minds boggled with information.
Mrs Ault chanted the answers out -
They all smudged into one big number.
Five, ten, fifty, one hundred.
That for an hour, then a carton of milk.
The puddles shimmer like glass from the autumn rain.
A bossy boy trips you up so you kick him.
Laughter is the language,
An older prefect rings the bell.
Shaking it furiously and we all scurry back to our classrooms.
The smell of ink, lead, wax and crayons hits you as you run
Into the classroom.
A meaningless tune on a keyboard made by another year group
Echoes through the corridors.
You feel the warm hand of your teacher pressing on your
Crumpled T-shirt - another sticker.
We were all so excited at the end of the day.
Who would be chosen to wipe today's work off the board?
Betrayal kicked in when you weren't chosen.
Home time!
You say, 'Bye!' to your teacher as she waves you off.
You stumble and fall, grazes on your battered knees.

Kathryn Boulter (14)
Sheldon School

Things I Would Miss

Tasty tomato ketchup on my chips,
The roaring of a car's engine driving away.
The feeling of soft, clean bed covers.
The amazing pages of a good magazine,
The wonderful smell of pizza in the oven,
The taste of a burnt, spicy bean burger with chilli sauce.
The silence of my dog running in a wheat field;
The rustling of autumn leaves,
The smell of petrol and
The taste of caramel and chocolate.

Tom Jenkinson (11)
Sheldon School

The Kittens

For kittens I had to wait and wait
And I finally got them slightly late,
Fozzy's a tabby, Pickle a tortie,
Both of them are extremely naughty.

When they first came they were very shy,
But they got used to us by and by,
Now as I try to get to sleep,
Cute little faces over covers peep.

Now I don't need any alarm,
Because Fozzy, not meaning any harm,
Comes and gently licks my nose,
While Pickle comes and nibbles my toes.

On their first visits outside,
They both ran in to go and hide,
Now we can hardly keep them away,
From going out to run and play.

But now when I see them in the flowers,
I am glad that they are ours.

Sarah Wade (12)
The Clarendon School

The Place Of The Souls

The graveyard sits outside the church
Empty, apart from a few dead souls,
Gravestones sunken by the sands of time,
Now no one comes to remember the dead.

This is a place of peace and remembrance,
Not for children to come and play,
Here you see glimpses of love and joy,
In the flowers that are changed each night.

Memories overgrown by time,
Like moss grows over these ancient stones,
The messages of love have faded away,
Only peace is alive here.

A quiet, special place to remember,
The lives of loved ones sadly lost,
The happiest times, the saddest times,
That others have long forgotten.

Kerena Sheath (11)
The Clarendon School

Graveyard Terror

Running through the fields,
Lurking through the mist,
I get to a spooky-looking graveyard,
A gust of wind lifts dust into my face.
The old trees swaying and creaking,
I come to a gravestone.
A shiver comes from my toes to my head,
Cobwebs are covering this gravestone.
I wipe the cobwebs away,
I look at the gravestone, it's marble,
With a picture, an old one of me!

Claire Louise Davies (11)
The Clarendon School

I Couldn't Do My Homework Miss

I couldn't do my homework Miss
It's quite simple really
A Russian man abducted me
And drowned me nearly!

I couldn't do my homework Miss
I don't know what I'm doing
My goldfish ate all of my books
And then it started mooing!

I couldn't do my homework Miss
We were injected with little ants
They ate all of my homework Miss
And then got in my pants!

The teacher tried to keep her cool
Trying not to be a fool
But in the end she swung him round
By his ears and soon she found
That shoving children down the loo
Jumping out and shouting, *'Boo!'*
Was all in all, a lot of fun
And all in all, had to be done
And this was all caused by one stupid boy,
Whose job was plainly to annoy
So don't get yourself in such a fiddle,
Just remember this good old riddle!

Jenny Egar (11)
The Clarendon School

My House

I live inside a very small house
With a great big white front door
My house is far too small to play
I don't want to live here anymore.
My garden is too small
I cannot play and run
I want a great big garden
To have lots and lots of fun.
My house is always noisy
There is always lots of noise
My little annoying brother screams and chucks his toys.
I want to grab him by the legs
And throw him down the stairs
But I know my mum will ground me
And that won't be very fair.

Daniel Pearson (11)
The Clarendon School

My Special Place

My special place, my special place,
Has got to be your big, warm face,
Your eyes, your smile might be the case,
Your face, your face, my special place.

My special thing, my special thing,
Has got to be my cygnet ring,
It might be that it makes a ping,
My ring, my ring, my special thing.

My special place, my special place,
Has got to be the outer space,
The moon, the stars, might be the case,
Space, space my special place.

Charlotte Robbins (12)
The Clarendon School

So Many People

So many people have died,
So many have cried.
I can't believe it's happened,
But it's not all over,
For there is so much more to be done,
Most of it without a gun.
So please don't cry
And don't let your faith die.

So many people have died,
So many have cried,
Bush and Tony have made these tears;
So many against, but they had no fears.
Saddam should be caught
And he should be taught,
That making lives hell is wrong
And he will suffer long,
But not as much as the people, whom he destroyed.

So many people have died,
So many cried,
It'll soon be over
And all we can do is hope for the best.

Ruth Bailey (12)
The Clarendon School

Blue Is The Colour

Blue is the colour,
Football is the game,
We're flippin' freezing
Cos we're watching in the rain.
Our team is naff
But we still remain,
Cos football, football is the game.

Andrew Sheppard (11)
The Clarendon School

Why Do We Have War?

War is damaging and hurtful,
War is a hurtful battle,
War is like a mad argument,
War kills honest people,
People made to do it,
Young people losing families.

Why do people like to hurt?
Only do it to win,
Why all the pain for something to own?
Why does this world need to fight?
Why does fighting need to kill?
Killing is regretful
Hurt and pain
Why do we destroy people now, today?

Why does it have to go on?
Why did it start all along?
People punishing people for something they've not done,
How has this world gone wrong?

Carly Stone (13)
The Clarendon School

Friends

F riends forever,
R eady to listen to your problems,
I n tough times, they'll cheer you up,
E ntrust them with your secrets,
N ever let you down,
D ependable, loyal and kind,
S o important!

Sophia Smith (11)
The Clarendon School

All Because Of You

Adults are dying,
Children and babies too,
Lying on the floor crying,
All because of you.
All their possessions left behind,
Ready to get bombed by you,
People going deaf and blind,
All because of you.
Saddam Hussein is running,
But you made up an excuse too,
You just keep the bombs coming,
All because of you.

Bombs flying everywhere,
Gas is turning blue,
Life just isn't fair,
All because of you.
You have killed many,
It's all of your army soon,
You say you haven't killed any,
All because of you.
You say the war is over,
But it's not and you know it too,
People have died and they will now suffer,
All because of you.

Angela Bunce (13)
The Clarendon School

Poems

P oetry is read every day,
O ne in a million, is excellent,
E veryone listening silently,
M agic atmosphere in the room,
S ilent bodies, sitting, waiting.

Rachel Kay (11)
The Clarendon School

The Lesson

It's such a bore,
I really must say it is a chore,
To sit all day,
While others go to play.

Lesson after lesson,
Hour to hour,
I sit and dread,
The lesson that leaves me almost half-dead.

From English to art,
And DT to ICT
Then after all this,
The lesson that kills bliss,
It's . . .

Monstrous maths!

Sadie-Louise Geen (11)
The Clarendon School

My Homework

Come and give me 50p
Oh I hate you Lee,
I can't do my work,
So leave me alone Mr Turck.

I left my homework on my bed,
Underneath my ted,
If you grabbed it, it would bite,
So I put up a fight.

As I went to do it,
I fell into a pit,
I also broke my wrist,
That wasn't on my list,
So I didn't do my homework in the end!

Katie Baker (11)
The Clarendon School

I Forgot To Feed The Cat!

I forgot to feed the cat
Because there's no cat food,
I'm sorry to the cat
I didn't mean to be so rude.

I forgot to feed the cat,
Because she wasn't at all hungry,
She begged and pleaded for no more,
Her belly must have been very low.

I forgot to feed the cat,
I thought the cat fed itself,
She was so quiet all of the day,
I really did think that she had gone away.

I forgot to feed the cat,
Because I forgot we had a cat,
She was so quiet all day long,
I didn't realise she was on the door mat.

Isabel Lucas (11)
The Clarendon School

Poems Are Hard

Poems are hard to write
One day I might
Write a poem that's good
Be cool that would
But I can't do it
I might just try and do a bit
But I can't think well
Maybe I should go to Hell
I don't know enough about writing
So I can just stay drawing fighting.

Nik Williams (12)
The Clarendon School

Rats And Pussycats

I like rats and pussycats,
Soft as a baby's bottom,
Black and white,
Like tiny zebras,
Or black and dark as night.

I like ones which are tame and live in houses,
Some are wild and roam the streets,
Some have long hair,
Others short,
Some have none at all!

I like playing with them,
They like string pulled along,
For them to chase,
Most of all I like it best,
When I hold them close to me.

Angela Wyatt (11)
The Clarendon School

7 Ways Of Looking At My Little Sister

A small glasses wearer, recorder player,
A strong, big built, football lover,
Bags of fun when in a good mood,
A ferocious, tom-boy,
A chocolate lover,
A kind, happy, loving sister,
A stubborn, outgoing, happy child.

Emma Hurren (11)
The Clarendon School

Destruction

Destruction and suffering are the effects of war,
How can anyone believe that war is the best, the true thing to do?
Innocent people crying, running, begging other humans,
Who are poised to kill them,
Others believe war is a reason to show your true colours,
Stand up for your leaders,
Gain them power,
Whether you lose a limb or your life,
Or cause other people to lose their lives for your
                              cause is purely up to you,
If you are one of these people,
Who doesn't care for others,
Think of their families, their loved ones,
If you have a conscience,
Think about the world's dream,
A world that's safe, a world of peace,
With no killing, pain or killing,
Everyone dreams of a world with no destruction.

Rachel Clare (12)
The Clarendon School

Lost Homework!

I really tried,
I really did,
I looked here
And I looked there,
I looked absolutely everywhere,
Please Miss just this once,
I'm really sorry, I really am,
A long silence hit the floor,
OK I'll do it again, I will.

Samantha Knight (11)
The Clarendon School

Alone

There stands a man,
Young and heartless,
There lies a child,
Cold and scared.

He hears voices shouting, ordering him around,
He lies there alone with a gun pointing at his face.

His family at home praying,
His family dead or imprisoned.

Everybody shouting,
Everybody moving,
Nobody caring,
Nobody listening.

Both alone!

Hannah Derrick (12)
The Clarendon School

No Homework!

Miss I really tried,
I left my homework so I cried,
I toasted and I fried,
I really, really tried,
Not to burn the bread.

Miss I really tried,
I left my homework so I cried,
Sorry, I got confused,
So I put my homework in the grill
And the toast in my bag.

Rianna Rose Lilly Ball (11)
The Clarendon School

Hallowe'en

The sun sets, darkness rises,
The moon high, wolves call,
Children dressed ready to trick or treat
Houses with pumpkins full of sweets.

Witches with brooms, hats and black cats,
Devils with horns, capes all in red,
Ghosts with black eyes all in white
Vampires with black capes, fangs ready for blood.

People wait for the knock at the door,
A full pot of sweets soon empty and dull
Houses decorated with spiders, pumpkins, cats
All the excitement for a scary night.

Hayley Naylor (11)
The Clarendon School

A Poem About Scrambling

S creaming through a muddy field,
C rashing over jumps and bumps,
R acing through the mud and rain,
A sking the bike to go once again,
M ud and dirt flying everywhere,
B ombing down hills, round corners and jumps,
L eaning over as you turn a corner,
I gniting up the long narrow straight,
N ot knowing what's lying around the corner,
G etting faster and faster and then slowing
    when there's a corner up ahead.

Paul Rush (11)
The Clarendon School

Me!

I'm small, I'm cool,
I'm not very tall,
I'm always climbing the school wall,
All the girls like me
And don't want to fight me,
Skateboarding's my hobby,
I do it all the time,
Mum knows where to find me,
When my time is done,
Whizzing through the air,
Like I just don't care,
All the girls watch me,
To see if I miss,
I wish!

Paul Ireland (11)
The Clarendon School

Best Friends

B est friends stick together,
E very day and forever,
S tay friends and never break up,
T reat them kindly and never make them sad.

F riends will never ever be nasty to each other,
R ebecca and Jordan will be friends forever,
I will always get new friends,
E veryone is my friend,
N othing can separate us,
D ays gone by but never argue,
S ouls are joint.

Rebecca Lanfear (11)
The Clarendon School

Smiling

Smiling is contagious,
You catch it like the flu,
I saw somebody today,
They smiled, so I did too.

Many people say it's fun
And I think that too
And people's teeth glow in the sun,
Oh what great smiles, they give you something to do.

My friends smile when I see them,
My family smile when I get home,
Everybody around makes a chain
Full of smiles all around the home.

Leah Coombs (11)
The Clarendon School

Grandma's Garden

In the garden, it's so fun,
Grandma's work is never done,
The things that glitter,
The things that shine,
Hang from the trees and twirl in time,
They never stop neither day nor night,
Even if the wind is light,
When the garden is full of flowers,
It makes me want to stay for hours,
In the winter, in the snow,
Grandma's garden has lost its glow.

Kimberley Jane Gee (11)
The Clarendon School

Happiness Is Important In Life

Happiness is important in life,
It's something that makes us want to smile,
It's like a tinkel from one to another,
When someone starts smiling, everyone joins in.

Everyone's been happy, some time in life,
Everyone's smiled more than once or twice,
Nobody's ever constantly smiling,
But nor are they constantly crying,
Most babies you see are sometimes crying,
But somewhere in them, happiness flows out.

Happiness is in the air all around us,
We breathe it in, then laugh it out,
So breathe a deep breath . . .
And smile!

Naomi Henry (13)
The Clarendon School

The Gas Attack

A shower of death covers us as we strain to reach our masks,
Thankfully I get mine on in time, but watch as others suffer,
People coughing and choking to death in a sea of pain!
It's not a nice sight but you experience it every day,
They choke, they die, they leave
And the next day I wonder, *will it be my turn?*
My turn from all the suffering?
I will have no family, no life, no nothing.

Robyn Hartley (12)
The Clarendon School

Question Of War

What's the point? What's the point?
What's the point in war?
Why they do it, nobody knows!
How they do it, do they really care?

They're not just people,
They call themselves 'me!'
What did they ever do?
Live, that's all, they're innocent.

The mess and destruction
They should be ashamed
'That's people's houses!'
They choose to destroy.

Do you really think,
If the innocent could turn
And do this to them,
That they'd like it?

Destroying their houses,
Taking their things,
Killing their family
And their friends.

All I can say is: what's the point? What's the point?
What's the point in war?
Why they do it, nobody knows!
How they do it, do they really care?

Rebekah Edwards (12)
The Clarendon School

Summer Is Late This Year

Summer is late this year, the skies are full of rain,
The garden soggy with water and there are puddles down the lane.
The breeze is cool, of the sun there is no sign, the
                              sky a deepening grey,
And the birds stay strangely silent, no summer here today.

The tiny plants are in the ground, and long to grow up strong,
But need the warmth of sunshine, to help them get along.
The fruit trees have lost all their flowers, and little fruits appear,
They need the sun's rays to bring them on, but
                              summer is late this year.

Holidays are booked down by the sea the children want to play,
But Mum fetches a colouring book, saying
                    'You had best stay in today!'
Later on to a leisure centre they all go, the swimming
                              pool gets the vote,
But not quite the same as being in the sea, in their little dinghy boat.

But wait! The sky is clearing, signs of blue are showing up high
And clouds that were so low and grey, have now gone floating by,
At last! A watery sun appears, oh! how a scene can change!
And hasty plans drawn up for the day, can now be rearranged.

The sun grows stronger, just feel the warmth!
The difference that it makes!
Already the sound of voices, around the boating lake.
And *splash!* there's someone in the sea!
Children start to play, don't waste your time,
Come join the fun, summer has come today!

Laura Price (11)
The Clarendon School

Smile At Me!

S mile for the camera,
M e smile, honestly,
I don't smile,
L augh and cry, scream and shout I can do that,
E veryone calls me Smiler and now you know why.

F rom ten years old,
O r even nine, I haven't smiled for a camera,
R eally, but no one believes me.

M aybe I can tell you a secret, I smile sometimes,
E veryone's got to smile sometimes,
    Everyone calls me Mini Lee and guess what,
    His nickname's Smiler too.

Stacey Hadley (11)
The Clarendon School

Freak!

October 31st, a night of scares,
Witches, devils, ghosts, nightmares,
Tricks or treats, fun to eat,
Parties and pumpkins.

When night-time is full,
No parties at all,
The real scares of Hallowe'en,
Awake to their own ghostly balls.

Rebecca Coles (12)
The Clarendon School

My Fairy Tale Poem

All fairy tales begin with - 'Once upon a time'
And finish with 'The End.'

Once upon a time a single man struck
Terror across millions of faces.

As children hid and prayed for their lives,
Adults fought and prayed for peace.

This man wasn't afraid and would do
Anything to prove it,
The people were afraid and would pay for it.

Now that man has been stopped,
But another has started.

There is no 'The End' to this fairy tale.
War isn't a fairy tale.

Kerry Hopper (12)
The Clarendon School

The Life Of The Bird

You started as an egg,
You came to life at midnight,
You didn't like your nest,
But who was to say,
You didn't like the rest,
Sadly now you must leave,
To seek life on your own,
But if you can't,
This will always be your home sweet home.

Aaron Osman (12)
The Clarendon School

The Black Statue

He stands there, his eyes upon us
Should we run away?
The sound of marching soldiers
Should we run or stay?

We rush and fumble to a sack,
To imitate the ground,
But there it stands bright and black,
Frozen to the sound
Of gunfire from the weapons of
The men from British ground.

They're running madly to escape
Or find a place to hide
I see a space it looks quite
Dark it's hidden to the side.

I run there
I won't look back
My feet are lead like bombs
The violence, the carnage
As our men are sent to tombs.

Hours pass, still I wait
Hidden in the dark,
The sound of soldiers falling,
Screaming like the lark.

They're leaving, I made it
The men from British ground
Our people are rejoicing
It's a very gracious sound.

Jack Muir (12)
The Clarendon School

Why?

You either kill or you die,
It's never our decision, only the killers.
But why?

Some say it's wrong, some say it's right,
Saddam or Bush, who to choose?
Still, never our decision.
But why?

The President of the United States of America,
He always says 'my people this' or 'my people that',
But actually it's all, me, me, me, me, me.
It's never our decision,
But why?

We think was it worth it?
All that pain and suffering to stop more
Pain and suffering,
It's never our decision,
But why?

The only thing we have a decision over is
What clothes to wear tomorrow or will
We win the football?
Never anything important,
But why?

Maybe Bush, Blair and Saddam
Should stop and look to see what they have done,
They won't, I know,
But it's still worth a try.

Hannah Greenman (12)
The Clarendon School

War

People crying,
People running,
People scattering,
Trying to hide,
Wondering when it's going to end.

People fighting for their lives,
People led on the ground,
Wondering if they're going to survive.

Is my life worth living after this?
I might as well be dead,
I don't want to live like this,
Everything is ruined,
Everything.

I can't take this anymore,
I just wish I was dead,
There's nowhere to run,
There's nowhere to hide,
Nowhere.

Emma Griffin-Banable (12)
The Clarendon School

Ice Cream

Strawberry, chocolate, mint and chip,
All very cold on my lip,
Vanilla as well in one big bowl,
Getting ready to gulp it whole,
Gooey lovely chocolate sauce,
Eat it for your second course.

Ashley Cradock (11)
The Clarendon School

My Little Bruv!

I really love
My little bruv
But rules have to be made,
I've had enough
You trash my stuff
My patience starts to fade!

My DVDs ain't Frisbees
I think you know the score
Don't pull my hair
Don't make me swear
Don't wee wee on the floor!

My lipsticks that I love to wear
Not pens to write on walls
My homework tidily done at night
You've screwed up in a ball!

You turn the TV on and off
You make awful smells
You chase the poor cat round the house
And pull it by its tail!

You climb up on the table
When I eat my tea
You wipe your nose in my clothes
You always aim for me!

You're sometimes such a little git
You fill me with dismay
But I really love you little bruv
More than I can say.

Kristy Dyson (11)
The Clarendon School

Homework

I really, really tried,
I was meant to pick it up,
I packed my bag ready for school,
I just forgot my homework.

I really, really tried,
I was walking to school,
When someone pushed me over,
Landed on my work and threw it in the bin.

I really, really tried,
I did it in the garden,
The dog was out playing,
I think he ate my homework.

I really, really tried,
I was about to do my homework,
When a big UFO landed outside,
They abducted me,
Sorry I really, really tried.

The teacher went red
And started to scream like a lion,
You've got a detention for a week,
So see you at my office at the end of school.

Tom Bartlett (11)
The Clarendon School

Skeleton

Hallowe'en is here,
Dressing up you are,
Trick or treating you go,
Knocking on people's doors.

Having lots of fun,
Walking around the street,
Scaring people as you go,
Tricking people as time goes on.

Gary Dell (11)
The Clarendon School

September 11th 2001

On September 11th 2001,
The Twin Towers fell down,
Millions of people got killed,
Parents, brothers, sister and all,
My uncle was one of these,
I hardly knew him at all,
I didn't find out until three days after,
But of course I was the first to know,
My uncle loved me very much,
He didn't know my brother,
He wasn't born when I saw him.

My auntie cried and cried and cried,
For two week's straight,
She came down to visit me,
But that didn't help much,
She went back to America and went straight back to her
Daughter and boyfriend,
She didn't stop crying until three weeks after,
When the funeral came, my auntie didn't go,
I didn't because I was too far away,
But that didn't stop me wishing I had.

Kirsty Adams (12)
The Clarendon School

Smelly Breath

There once was a woman called Steff
Who had really bad-smelling breath
She had minging teeth
And liked eating beef
Her breath was as lethal as death.

Ryan Spong (11)
The Clarendon School

It's A Cruel World

War is bad, war is wrong,
As it kills those innocent ones,
The ones who have done nothing at all,
The ones that just pay their way through life
And this is what they get, it's not deserved.

I think the Iraq war was right though,
As Saddam Hussain was cruel,
He treated his people as if they were worth nothing,
Saddam Hussein should be touched with grief,
Saddam Hussein is the one worth nothing.

The cruel things that happen in wars,
Are when very young children are lost in tears,
They lose their parents and family,
And are left all alone, cold and hungry,
All they can do is sit, frightened and scared, until found.

Wars are worthless, and cause so much damage,
They ruin people's lives, yet sometimes make them better,
The Iraq war is one symbol of happiness,
Now he is gone and left the country, life can live on,
And all those people who were in pain
Can now move on.

Louise Allberry (12)
The Clarendon School

Love

Love is red like a newly spring rose
Love smells like a scented candle,
When you are in love,
You can hear fireworks going off,
Love makes you feel soft and warm inside,
You can see the firework display,
Love lives deep inside of you.

Kelly Ellis (11)
The Clarendon School

My Dog Called Jamie

Jamie eats
What he can find
Edible
He doesn't mind.

Socks, pants, anything,
Playfulness,
Will make him spring.

In a while,
Watch your plate,
Cos dog's tea is
Never late.

Whatever you have,
He doesn't care,
As long as you will
Always share.

At walkie time,
He likes to run,
Tricks for treats,
Is always fun.

If you don't know, who he is yet,
You should now cos he's my pet.

The springer spaniel always wins!
Just look past his dirty sins!

Naomi Lowson (11)
The Clarendon School

Gerry The Giraffe

There was a giraffe called Gerry
Who really liked to eat berries,
He ate the wrong sort,
Oh no's what he thought
Next time I think I'll eat cherries.

Hannah Phillips (11)
The Clarendon School

War Is Eternal

On the dust encrusted plain
It is clear there is no fame
On the bloody field
All war can be is eternal greed
Shooting, blasting and through all
Evil is among us all,
Among us all.

Matthew McLaughlin (12)
The Clarendon School

As Red As . . .

As red as
a red rose growing
in the garden.

As red as
Mars spinning around
the universe.

As red as
a tomato lying in the
salad bowl.

As red as
gory blood dripping
from your arm.

As red as
holy berries hanging
from the Christmas tree.

As red as
a sparkling ruby
on a young woman's ring.

And that is what I think of
when I see red.

Douglas Rose (13)
The Cotswold Community School

Murder In The Night

M urder in the night.
U nderneath the moonlight flowing through the window
R esting on their deep feathered pillow,
D efenceless, unknowing the atrocity awaiting - the victims sleep.
E ach minute darkness gathers close,
R eaching for the door.

I nto the light the guilty steps
N o features just an outline, a shadow.

T he figure enters, swift, no sound.
H elpless the victims sleep,
E vil, a gleam of silver.

N ext to the door he stands and,
I n the impenetrable gloom,
G athers beside the bed.
H e raises high, the gleaming silver . . .
T hief. He has just stolen their lives.

Daniel Blackmore (15)
The Cotswold Community School

Fire

Fire, fire dancing in the snow,
Whipping, lashing at the air,
Like a tongue of fury,
Never stopping,
Never knowing,
When it's going to pounce,
Then the silence,
Of the charcoal,
Burning in defiance,
As it gets washed away.

Jake Simmonds (12)
The Cotswold Community School

Bad Is Good

Oh felonies we make
Oh terror we create
If we get caught, we won't have a last resort
So terrible we feel
Not a chance to heal
We get put in jail
To live and frail
We all have a good side
Even if we don't oblige
Bad is good to live forever
Bad is good, good is bad
Bad is good.

Joshua Robinson (12)
The Cotswold Community School

Strange

All I see is empty,
All I see is shapes,
All I see is dark,
All I see is strange.

All I see is evil,
All I see is sad,
All I see is wired,
All I see is strange.

All I see is light,
All I see is life.

What is life?
Just strange.

Cameron Picton (14)
The Cotswold Community School

The Will To Live

Each morning when I wake up I feel so down
Don't want to face the faces that taunt me
As I try to work up courage and free my thoughts of them
They always come back to haunt me
Life never asked me what I wanted
But I know what answer I would give
If I got asked that question
I'd want the free will to live
Why do people put others down because they're different?
Our confidence is not a toy for them to break
Many children suffer alone in silence
But I've done that and it's not the path to take
Crying in your room when others are happy
Making no sense of all the hurt you feel in your heart
Trying hard not to show what they're doing to you
But really they have pulled you apart
Don't toss and turn in bed at night
Don't run away from the pain
I know you think no one feels what you feel inside
But many others go through this strain
Your head is full of questions
And you are feeling so depressed
With nobody to talk to
Feeling in agony, bruised and distressed
You feel like you are a prisoner
Bound and broken in chains
But I have been there where you are
And I'll be with you next time it rains.

April Walker
Westwood St Thomas CE School

The Gate

Standing in the lychgate
echoing my screaming hate
lifeless words carved in wood
to which we misunderstood
a chasm of cobwebs I battle
breaking the silk as I fall
stand beneath the eerie arch
shatter each muscle in my heart
catch me tumbling from a web
turn and run away instead
this place is a destiny
the dead are always free
think of those whose gift it is
steal the silence in a kiss
the darkness here sets in
the dead come here to sing
we fear the light turning off
where will I run?
When will I stop?

Tasha Glew (15)
Westwood St Thomas CE School

Tears

I stood there looking down,
I wondered where you looking back?
My eyes filled with tears,
As I thought of the past.
I recalled the memories that had been put to rest
The falls were upsetting,
The trips were the best.
I laid flowers down, as I tore through the grass
I struggled reading your name,
While in the sky, birds passed.
Little did they know what I felt like, as I stared?
The emptiness, the loneliness,
And the nights when I felt bare.
That was almost a year ago -
The tears have nearly gone,
Although I'll never forget you
I know that I have to move on.

Suzi Milne
Westwood St Thomas CE School

I Flew To The Moon

I flew to the moon
In a very big balloon.
All I wanted was to see it
Not to land on it.
Now I'm stuck here all alone.
Now all I want is to go home.
I'm stuck here all alone
And I just want to go home.

Daniel Robinson (12)
Wootton Bassett School

Somme

The metal monsters roar,
Fire spewing from their mouths,
They are hungry and we must feed them.
We feed them cold metal,
In seconds this metal will hammer down,
Onto the hounds of Hell.

The bounds of Hell are just like me,
They are afraid, tired and hungry
Just like me.
They fear our monsters as we fear theirs.
But we have no choice,
We must fight.

We are safe from the bullets that buzz like wasps
It is the men on the frontline that die,
They drown in puddles of mud and blood.
My friends have died
Because the bullets tore through their tender flesh.

The empty, barren lands are destroyed
With a few men around
We are all alone.
I can sense death is coming,
It will be swift and soon,
Every night I wonder if I will
See the sunset again.

But still I will fight this pointless war
For I will serve my king and country
My monster is the only thing that keeps
The hounds of Hell away.

Mark Lazenby (15)
Wootton Bassett School

Fermentation

We all ferment, a face can change, but souls stay young,
Don't take me down, because I'm not done,
Don't steal my crown, before it's won,
Just because of all the things I've done,
The wheel of chance will turn back my way,
The sky will not be grey any more.

I don't want to be
Like other people are
Don't want to own a key
Don't want to wash my car
Don't want to have to work
Like other people do
I wanted to be free
I wanted to be true
Don't want to wake at night
Or wait until it's light
I wanted to be free
I thought that I was right.

We all ferment, tastes can change, but the past stays young,
Don't you know that I'm here beside you?
Can't you see that I can't relax?
When I saw you in my rear view
You could have stopped me in my tracks.

We all ferment, the past stays young, but the future changes,
I wanted to be free, I wanted to be true, I thought that I was right;
I thought that you were right,
Yet it only seems just like yesterday
We used to run and hide
Remember in the park where we used to play
The grass looked ten foot high.

We all ferment, we all change, and I thought
That you were right; I thought that I was right . . .

James Rowell (15)
Wootton Bassett School

Moving House

I shall not notice the difference,
The stair that creaks as soon as you touch it,
The bathroom floor that creaks like a mouse.
The mini-corridor out of my room with walls so
Close you can climb up like a monkey and
Nudge the wooden board that is the attic 'door'.

I shall not notice the difference;
My warm radiator and smooth curtains.
The curtains that you can hide behind in the lounge.
The massive space that is our garden,
Blue tits flying in and out,
Eating their fill of seed.

After all I have said so far,
A denial;
I *shall* notice the difference.

Katherine Wilson (11)
Wootton Bassett School

Autumn Storm

Tucking up in the chilly sky
Amber and peach way up high
The crisp crimson descendants fall from the hands
Of the largest oak in the land
Listen, listen friend of she
We see no more that busy bee
The pretty flowers of the ground
No longer make that happy sound
The cupboards fill with large fluffy coats
The sea deserted with no more boats
I sit in bed all nice and warm
And forget about the autumn storm.

Lauren Ratcliffe (11)
Wootton Bassett School

My Mum

Being my mum is a difficult job,
That's not always easy to do,
Finding my washing, washing my washing,
Ironing my clean clothes without burning them too.

When I come home from school trying to find
Something to do for you,
Looking in the sink for some dirty dishes
But they're already washed, sparkling clean by you.

So take a rest for once in your life,
I'm sure it won't do you no harm,
I will tidy up I'll find all my laundry for you,
I'll try to work out how to use the washing machine,
I'll wash the laundry but they might turn pink.

So please, please take a rest on your birthday,
Now it's time to raise your glasses to my mum
The No 1 Mum, the best mum in the whole world
One more thing I would like to say is to my mum
I love you!

Hannah Day (11)
Wootton Bassett School

An Autumn Poem

A mber carpets in every dew-covered garden
U nder every costume a kid is yelling trick or treat or eating sweets
T he giant statues have shaken off their brown gloves
U nder the statues, people watch the bluey purple sunset
M ums and dads begging children not to eat all the
                                        Hallowe'en sweets,
N asty bugs crawling under the ground.

Daniel Jupe (11)
Wootton Bassett School

Not An Ending!

I did not feel the pain,
As I fell and broke my wrist,
I did not feel the pain,
As I had it put in plaster,
I did not feel the pain,
As it was being removed,
I did not feel the pain,
It didn't hurt!

I did not understand,
How I fell and broke my wrist,
I did not understand,
Why I had it put in plaster,
I did not understand,
Why it was being removed,
I did not understand,
It didn't hurt!

Allanah Skuse (11)
Wootton Bassett School

Suffering

I hear screaming, groaning, rustling,
I feel starvation, fear, worrying,
This is where I live,
All take and no give,
Even with people, I feel alone,
I live here, with such a dull tone,
I feel scared for all my life,
I might not survive to have a wife,
Endless rows of ill people,
See them dying, poor people,
Some dying, some mild,
But all I am is just a child.

Edward Sanger (12)
Wootton Bassett School

My Fears

My fears are of monsters
Underneath my bed
Coming out at night
Eating me up whole.

My fears are of earthquakes
In the middle of the day
Buildings falling down
Burying us alive.

My fears are of car crashes
On the motorway
Some of the people get killed
Though some of us survive.

My fears are of war
People getting killed
There's no need for war
War should not exist.

Our world is full of fears
Whichever way you look
You have a fear
As well as them and I.

So do not sit and ponder
Just carry on and go
About your daily life
As though they don't exist.

Susanne Slade (13)
Wootton Bassett School

My Poem

On a dark autumn night
I can hear no children fight
Sparkling webs shine through the light
On that dark autumn night.

On a sunny summer's day
The sun would shine all the day
I would hear the children play
On that sunny summer's day.

On a frosty autumn eve
I could taste a chilly breeze
I could see the raindrops freeze
On that frosty autumn eve.

On a windy autumn day
The sky is stuck in a dull grey
People freeze and work all day
On that windy autumn day.

Libby Birnie (11)
Wootton Bassett School

Autumn

Autumn is here, winter is coming,
Spring and summer have come and gone,
Trees stand tall, their wooden fingers stretching
Out to the blue sky above,
As we walk through the woods, the rustling
Leaves under our feet,
The sun is setting, the day is ending,
The night is getting closer until it hits,
The cold night air blowing ferociously,
The frosts come to murder all the beautiful flowers,
As the animals sleep in their warm beds,
Until the day when the sun is shining again.

Emily Bourne (11)
Wootton Bassett School

Autumn

Autumn is
Blowing the summer diet
End of season bargains, I must buy it.

Autumn is
Reading the forgotten book,
I was only going to take a look.

Autumn is
Being together
Praying for warm weather.

Autumn is
Drinking hot cocoa
Looking through the family photos.

Autumn is
Snuggling down in bed
Thoughts of Christmas running through my head!

Amber Heath (11)
Wootton Bassett School

Being Bullied

People tease you, nowhere to go
Nowhere to hide,

No friends to be there, not one person cares,

People stare at you as if you look strange,

You're too scared to talk
You're too scared to walk,

People punch you and kick you,
They don't care,
They won't care,
They're bullies.

Charlotte Matthews (11)
Wootton Bassett School

My Family

My family makes me smile,
Me being born was worthwhile,
We laugh and play,
Nearly every day.

Nothing seems to go wrong,
Unless Dad's got his golf on.

Weekends are good,
We play in hail and snow,
Mum always joins in,
Unless she goes to bingo.

Charlotte works on a Saturday morning,
She gets up as the sun is dawning,
When she gets home she feels so proud,
Oh my goodness what's that noise?
My sister's music is so loud!

I love my family very much,
We have a good laugh that's a good touch,
We will always be friends together,
In the present, the future and forever.

Sammy Oliver (12)
Wootton Bassett School

Sunshine

When the sun comes up to start the day,
We all shout out hip, hip, hooray,
Then when we're in the midday sun,
We love having loads and loads of fun,
The end of the day, the sun goes down,
We all give a sigh and a little frown,
So when we go home, we think of the fun,
Just can't wait till the morning sun.

David Collett (13)
Wootton Bassett School

Best Friends!

(Dedicated to Jillian Kelly)

No matter how many friends you have,
100, 50, 9 or 2,
There will always be one who will stick by you,
She may be blonde, she may be brown,
She may be thin, she may be round,
But what you don't know is behind her face,
Is what she is thinking of a lonely place,
You should be there to help her in need
And never disrespect her because of some greed,
You may fall out over silly things,
Like boys and make-up, recent flings,
A true best friend will never judge
And if we fight, won't hold a grudge,
I'll wear her clothes,
She'll do my hair
And if I'm upset,
She'll always be there
And when I'm old and bent and grey,
Her friendship will still light my way,
We'll not need gold or mink or pearls,
Cos we're best friends and we're
'The Girls!'

Lara Hawkins (12)
Wootton Bassett School

True Love

One day I thought I knew
The reason for me and you,
Forever we stay together
For our love I know is true
That way it will always stay
Forever till we part
My love will always stay
Within the edges of your heart.

Jade Roulstone (12)
Wootton Bassett School

I Used To . . . But Now I . . .

I used to drink coffee, but now I have tea,
I used to like Brussels sprouts, but now I prefer peas,
I used to be scared of the dark, but now I am brave,
I used to get in trouble, but now I can behave.

I used to have curly hair, but now it is straight,
I used to go to bed early, but now I stay up late,
I used to like waking up, but now I stay in bed,
I used to play basketball, but now it's badminton instead.

I used to miss my coach to school, but now I catch them all,
I used to be really tiny, but now I am quite tall,
I used to have crooked teeth, but now they're all in place,
I used to play the electric guitar, but now I play the bass.

I used to leave my room in a mess, but now it's sorted out,
I used to stay at home all day, but now I'm out and about,
I used to be a toddler, but now I'm in my teens,
I used to like pink and red, but now it's blues and greens.

Lisa Turner (13)
Wootton Bassett School

Chance

How can you sleep at night
Knowing people have to live in filth and dirt?
And maybe not waking up, just trying
To reach out for a little faith to
Carry them on for a few more days.
The silent cries in everyone's eyes,
Just waiting to die of hunger,
We should feel guilty, that we
Are standing back doing nothing.
So next time you moan and cry
About not having any sweets,
Think twice,
These people don't even have
A chance to live!

Sophie Lattimer (12)
Wootton Bassett School

Bullies

The skin that you bear,
Whatever you wear,
The style of your hair,
Can't be who you are.

Short-sighted or not,
They won't face the truth,
Judgements made,
Tears through your life.

It's hard,
I know,
Like living in Hell.
I've seen.

If only they didn't stare,
And it didn't hurt
When they glared.

Take heart,
One day they'll see
Nothing was gained,
Only misery.

Hope sustained,
You're free now
From all the pain,
And you're all that remains.

Gaby Sharma (12)
Wootton Bassett School

In Parting

A smile I offered you in parting.
Lingers. Like a forgotten scent.
In the afternoon you went, a shadow of a memory,
A whisper of old love.
My shoes scrape along the concrete,
My footfalls ringing out behind hem,
Are a blasphemy in the silence.
Grey fingers part the sky, sunlight peers through,
Weak, faded, but constant.
The breeze ruffles your hair, black it shines in the dawn.
You are a ghost, a spectre, a happy dream,
The wind blows and you are gone.
I heard you last night, crying again.
Your tears lie along your face, they mark the sadness,
Stain your cheek.
All I can do is sit there, waiting for the storm to pass.
What's wrong? I never seem to ask.
I heard you crying last night, but then it stopped,
And so had you.

Daniel Hardy (16)
Wootton Bassett School

Autumn Is . . .

Autumn is a cuddly teddy bear tickling your chin,
Autumn is a child splashing through puddles.
In autumn, jewels nestle in the grass.
It's a dusty room with light only from a small window.
Autumn is an old man laughing, laughing,
Autumn is a glass gleaming in the light.
It's a child's soft breathing in the depth of the night.
Autumn is a baby splashing in a pool,
Though autumn is nice, winter is cruel.

Kyra Edgington (11)
Wootton Bassett School

One Night

At half-past nine
You hear the clock chime
Leaves rustling in the wind
Movements of animals outside
Humans walking with a stride
The lights switch off
The dark is all around
You hear the barking of a greyhound
Children crying
Elderly sighing
The wind is wailing
The tree is failing
You hear strange sounds
But nothing's been found
You wake up in the morning
Stretching and yawning
Forgetting about the night before
Then you know tonight
You will have to go through the gore again!

Steven Carr (12)
Wootton Bassett School

Autumn

Autumn is something that is like a day by the fire
Drinking hot chocolate.
My favourite plate of soft pancakes which are yum!
Watching my favourite TV soap till late.
Staring out of the window, seeing birds building a nest.
Coming from outside, it's lovely to hear the leaves rustling on the floor
And the bright brown conkers falling on the muddy ground.
I like autumn, it makes things come back to me.

Kayleigh Skinner (11)
Wootton Bassett School

The Rose

He picked me a rose,
From his mother's prized bunch.
He kissed me
And told me
It was a symbol of his love.

A week passed,
The rose began to wither.
My father said,
'That's a sign, that is.'
But I ignored him.

Another week flew by,
The rose looked really sad.
I looked out of the window,
Waiting for hours,
He did not come.

I turned to the rose,
Full of anger and fear.
I wanted it to tell me
Where he was.
Why was he not here?

I turned back to the window.
I saw him get out
Of his new car.
With another girl!
I began to scream.

With anger and with hate
Boiling inside of me,
I turned to my dead rose
And flung it on the fire,
And watched the symbol burn.

Caitlin Smith (13)
Wootton Bassett School

Jack And Mary

Once upon a storm
A terrible storm
In a little wooden house sat he.
And across from him
In a little ragged dress
On a little narrow bed sat she.

He cursed and he swore
And her little swollen cheek
Bore the marks of his latest abuse.
Her little frozen hands held
A heavy china plate
And her trembling little feet marched on.

She stopped just before him
Silent tears on her cheeks
And she curtseyed, laying down his dinner as she did.
And if it wasn't cooked right
His big wooden stick
Came out and beat her head.

She scrubbed the pots and pans
And tidied up the room,
But suddenly his best glass slipped out of her hand.
The quiet little crash
Was followed by his roar
And she tensed her body and waited.

His stick across her head came again and again
But this time she didn't rise.

He realised she was dead and let out a howl.
Stumbled out of the door - into an unseen bog.
Never seen again.

Kerry Pearson (13)
Wootton Bassett School

Autumn

A man sat on a bench,
With his grandsons around him,
'Let me tell you,
What I remember of autumn.

Autumn reminds me of
The orange flames of the fires,
Flickering in front of my face,
Safe and sound,
Snug and warm.

Autumn reminds me of
The dark nights,
Stars glinting,
The fog and mist,
Swirling me up through the sky.

Autumn reminds me of
The crackling bonfires,
Smoke rising up to the greyish night,
Fireworks shooting, zooming,
Swirling round and round,
Blazing my eyes with light.

Autumn reminds me of
The setting sun,
Pink streaking the sky,
The blustery wind,
Whirling, swirling, round my body.

Boys playing conkers,
Girls stirring the golden leaves.'
He gazed in wonder,
His eyes closed
Against the modern world,
Wrapped in his own thoughts.

Rebecca Foxwell (11)
Wootton Bassett School

The Walk To School

As I was going to school one day,
I was full of the joys of spring.
Then I tripped, I fell - oh blow
I felt my knickers go ping.

I looked around feeling a fool
Thinking, *what on earth can I do?*
I grabbed my skirt with all my might
- I looked down - they were there by my shoe.

There, for the world to see
I was pink with embarrassment and shame.
I couldn't pretend that they weren't mine,
And stamped all over them - was my name!

I heard a voice come towards me,
I couldn't believe my bad luck.
It was Cole, the coolest guy in the world,
God! This day really sucks!

I ran and ran as fast as I could
Then I remembered - my bottom was bare!
What do I do? I can't go back
Oh this day just isn't fair!

All I could do was to go and hide
Behind the big oak tree
I watched as Cole looked around
Oh my god! He's calling for me!

I couldn't believe it - I gasped in shock
There was Cole - hiding a snigger.
He handed to me - what I thought was a note -
I looked down - and there were my knickers!

Amy Shailes (12)
Wootton Bassett School

Friends

Friends are very helpful to me,
they help me in every way,
they help me when I am sad and ill
and when I am stuck.

Friends are very important in everyone's life,
if we had no friends we would feel very alone.
They play with us,
and give us good advice.

They are like a second family to us,
if you had no friends,
you would feel like
you were in a big black hole.

Jade Stivala (11)
Wootton Bassett School

9/11 - It Never Happened

I
was not
there, I did
not see or
hear or even
smell. I did not
pray, I did not cry.
I did not crumple, or
want to die. I did not
know what happened,
neither how and where. I
don't know who it happened
to and I don't even care. I did
not wipe a tear, I did not brush
their hair. I do not need it, no. So
don't stand there,
run away and
go!

Sophie McFarlane (12)
Wootton Bassett School

My Dog

My dog loves to play ball
And roll around on the floor,
He has white fluffy fur
And when he runs he becomes a blur.
He loves going for walks
And eating roast pork,
But you should never doubt
That he will get gravy all over his snout.
He loves chasing cats
But has never seen a rat,
He likes sleeping on my bed
But needs a pillow for his head.
He also sleeps on the floor
In his basket and behind the door.
He is a dog everyone adores
He is a dog no one can ignore,
Without fail
He will greet you with a wagging tail.
That's my dog Sparky!

Rebecca Dudley (11)
Wootton Bassett School

Autumn

Autumn reminds me of Hallowe'en
When vampires come out to haunt you,
When skeletons tumble out of towering cupboards.
Autumn reminds me of dew
Thrown on our grass by the sky,
Petals floating gently down to their grave.
Autumn reminds me of my dad's,
My friend's and my birthday.
Thank you autumn!

Laura Knapp (11)
Wootton Bassett School

Autumn

Autumn days,
When I can't get out of bed,
The rich red and golden brown leaves,
The cold chill I dread.

Hallowe'en is near,
Just after that it's Bonfire Night,
Everyone wraps up nice and warm,
I stand and watch the bright sparkling lights.

Conkers dropping on the ground,
Acorns scattered around your feet,
Animals hibernating in their homes,
The winter is near and Christmas too.

People walk past you with red beaming faces,
The strong wind brushes through your hair,
All the other seasons are brilliant as well,
But autumn has something special!

Kirsty Stanley (11)
Wootton Bassett School

School Fun

S chool, school, school,
C loser than you expect,
H ours you spend there,
O r maybe you forget,
O ranges or packet lunch,
L emons for your drink, or even
S our apples in your new school bag.

F un at breaktime,
U nhappy at lunch,
N aughty, naughty, detention for you next lunch.

Jason Foster (13)
Wootton Bassett School

Autumn Reminds Me Of . . .

Autumn reminds me of . . .
When my dog Mouse sleeps in his bed
When nobody is at home.

Toasting by the fire,
On a cold night
Watching the flames through the glass.

Seeing the crystal-coloured raindrop
Falling quickly into the deep depths of the canal.
Seeing the rippling effect on the water's surface.

These are things
That remind me of the autumn times.

But also the leaves fall off the trees.
Wind blows fierce and everything looks dull and frosty
One thing is that it is nearly . . . *Christmas!*

Amiee Simpkins (11)
Wootton Bassett School

Autumn

Autumn is like a hot cup of cocoa,
Warm and chocolatey in your tummy,
Autumn's air so clean and fresh,
Taste the mist in the cool sky,
See the kites fighting with the wind,
Children snug in their beds,
Mums and dads give a warm kiss,
To their children to help them drift off to sleep,
Now autumn sleeps and winter awakens.

Sophie Dow (11)
Wootton Bassett School

Oasis

Child of light, child of life,
Green power blooming in the desert sand.
Blazing emerald, blazing sun,
Shimmering fire across the water.

Time of life, stretch of light,
Bearing you on to the horizon,
And beyond.
Trick of the eyes, trick of the light,
And the emerald life is gone again.

Long have I roamed, searching the sand,
Lest the emerald light shine on me again.
For eternity, I shall wander these ways,
Lost as the desiccated ancient bones.

For the search is eternal, yet we are not,
Fragile as glass, or a deadly green mirage,
I shall wander as long as my body can stand,
Wander here amidst the desert sand.

And when I crumble,
Fall,
And stumble,
The emerald life alone shall remain.

Tim Cruise (16)
Wootton Bassett School

I Want To Know

There's so many things I want to know
From the sky to the rainbow even with the snow.
They say the earth came from a big bang
They say the earth came from God
But which one is it?
I really want to know.
There's so many things I want to know
From the sky to the rainbow even with the snow.
How was I farmed?
Could I have been once a little crow?
I really want to know.
There's so many things I want to know
From the sky to the rainbow even with the snow.
When I grow older
Will I be beautiful like now?
Or will I have wrinkles with a frown?
I really want to know.
There's so many things I want to know
From the sky to the rainbow even with snow.
When I die
Will I be an angel or a devil?
Will I go to Heaven or Hell?
I really want to know.
There's so many things I want to know
From the sky to the rainbow even with the snow
There's so much more but who will tell
I really want to know!
There's so many things I want to know
From the sky to the rainbow even with the snow!

Holly Jones (12)
Wootton Bassett School

She's Gone

The day she went,
I didn't hate it,
I didn't stand there crying,
Steadily like rain,
Mourning her passing.
In the days that came,
I didn't miss her arms,
Cuddling me close,
Her voice soft and gentle,
Telling me she loved me.
I won't miss her smell
Of mint and her perfume.
Her eyes shining blue
And unblinking when telling her stories
I won't miss them
I won't miss her
I won't miss her.

Hayley Grover (12)
Wootton Bassett School

The Vulcan

She handles like a pearl
Thunders through the sky
As it passes over, the wind roars towards me
It makes my bones shake.

I get so nervous as it turns around
The smell in the air makes me sweat
It smells of petrol and burning.

It looks like an arrowhead aiming for me
Its silver skin shines in the sun
I wish I could fly one but now they're all gone
And stick to the ground forever.

Alexander Weston (11)
Wootton Bassett School

My Guardian Angel

(Dedicated to my guardian angels,
Lara Hawkins, Sophie Lattimer and Holly Moffat)

When I sleep, you protect me,
All through the day,
You, I can't see,
But you can see me,
You watch, protect and love,
You are my guardian angel,
Sent from above,
Sent down to watch over me,
Sent down to care,
Sent down to bring life,
Sent down to share,
To share your wisdom, knowledge and love,
Because you, my guardian angel,
Were sent from above.

Jillian Kelly (12)
Wootton Bassett School

Bravado

I make you think that you're the best,
I make you think you rule the rest,
I make you think you are so smart,
I make your teacher fly through the sky,
Because your test marks are so high,
I make your friend who thinks she's smart
Look like a silly tart,
When your mum asks you a question,
You give her a long suggestion,
She says, 'Gee whizz, I asked a question,'
But now I'm gone, I'm fed up of you,'
'You're silly being smart,'
I think you'd be better off as a tart.

Rebecca Munton (11)
Wootton Bassett School

Vanity - I Love My . . .

I love my eyes
I love my hair
I love my nose
I love to share

I love my mouth
I love my ears
I love my attitude
I love my tears

I love my toes
I love my face
I love my brain
I love my brace

All these things say I love me
This is called vanity.

Christina Taylor (11)
Wootton Bassett School

Autumn Days

Autumn days are cold and windy.
When the leaves are falling on the green, lush grass
the dew soaks through the dry, crunchy leaves.

When you wake up in the morning
and it's 7 o'clock and it looks like it's 5 o'clock
you think, *why am I up?*

As the wind bows it whistles through the gap of the door.
At night you look at the stars and they're bright at sight.

Lauren Smith (11)
Wootton Bassett School

Autumn

Autumn is a rundown shed
whose hinges are frost-bitten.

Autumn is a time of warmth and love,
a cosy fire to snuggle up to.

Autumn is the birds, fleeing to find
their new home before the cold takes them.

Autumn is a ship setting sail,
never to dock again.

Autumn is a raggedy tramp with no home to go to
and no one to cherish him.

Autumn is toasted crumpets,
crunchy and warm.

Autumn is hot chocolate,
hot and soothing.

Autumn is a time to cherish
while you can.

Andrew Ware (11)
Wootton Bassett School

Autumn

Autumn days,
Paw prints in the snow.
But as soon as it rains,
They all start to go.

Long, long nights,
I'm snuggled up in bed.
All the Christmas thoughts
Are floating in my head.

Car decided not to start,
Conkers in the way.
Leaves fluttering all about,
Autumn's the best, I have to say!

Chelsea Harris (11)
Wootton Bassett School

Autumn

Autumn reminds one of earmuffs,
warm and snug
and one's home, safe and sound.

It reminds me of a TV,
funny and entertaining
and people lying in their beds,
dreaming peacefully.

It reminds one of tea and cocoa,
tasty and relaxing
and of a soldier, standing his ground.

It reminds one of treats and sweets.
luscious and thoughtful
and of love, precious and fragile.

Iain Robert Ferguson (11)
Wootton Bassett School

Equal Chances

Britain is a multicultural nation
Made of people of every denomination
Free to pursue their religion of choice
Safe in the knowledge that they have a voice.

But few can't take this
And try to dismiss
The fact that we're equal
And now here's the sequel.

Others may look weird
And have a furry beard
But we can do things the same
The only difference is our name.

Michael Ford (14)
Wootton Bassett School

Winter

I can wipe out whole species,
With just a simple touch,
I can decorate the windows,
Making them glimmer and dance with joy.

I am the season of coldness,
Death and spitefulness too.
I am the most powerful of seasons,
For I can bring love and joy.

I am the friend of no one
And I care for no one in return.
I despise everything ever made,
But summer is the worst of all.

My life is nothing but despair,
It is like a nightmare that never ends.

Gwennie Hopkins (11)
Wootton Bassett School

A Friend's Prayer

May your dreams bring you;

The answers to your deepest questions,
The possibilities of all you can do,
The wisdom to know your right pathways,
The guidance to make your visions come true.

The loyalty to keep your promises safe,
The faith to confide in your greatest friend,
The confidence to find your real self,
The love and trust which never ends.

Kim Rayner (11)
Wootton Bassett School

There Is No Pain Inside Me

You don't lie in every inch of my heart,
I sleep at ease, no thought of you,
No tears speared as you're deceased,
I was not vexed at your death,
Just no sorrow when they lowered
You into the ground,
There was no pain as the ground
Swallowed you up,
All that's left are visions of your loving eyes,
I feel no pain.

As days go by you were blocked out of
My life,
No minute or second did I think of you.
When I sit at your grave no happy memories
Run into my mind,
Watching loved ones cry every night
But I stand in high morals
No pain to be felt
I feel no pain.

Liam Rowe (13)
Wootton Bassett School

Autumn

Autumn is when you're in your house
and you're feeling bored.
Autumn is when you're feeling ill
and you're taking tablets with your mum.
Autumn is when it's feeling chilly
so you're sitting in front of the fire.
Autumn is when your dad is in front of the TV
eating pancakes with melted butter on top.
Autumn is cool.

Tom Doherty (11)
Wootton Bassett School

Despair!

I don't care what you did to me,
you didn't hurt me at all
when you hit me against the cold wall.

I never knew why, although I don't care
your wish for me to die
as you pulled my long blonde hair.

You hit me all the time,
you never seemed placid,
shouting and cursing I knew you were on acid.

I never care, I never will
as you stare back with your expressionless face,
I wonder what the court would say about this case?

I explore your eyes, nothing I can see
your face seems dead,
you mean nothing to me.

As I sit shivering against the wall
I hate you and never loved you,
I feel so small.

Kathryn Dixon (14)
Wootton Bassett School

Spite

I love winding the neighbours up
Playing loud music wakes them up.
Police came knocking on the door
Telling me not to do it anymore.
I shut the door and said, 'Yeah right,'
What they gonna do, put up a fight?
The neighbour comes round and gives me a slap
I do the same and slap her back.
Everywhere I go and everything I do
Spite just seems to follow me through!

Amber Brown (11)
Wootton Bassett School

Autumn Is . . .

Autumn is thunder,
Making dogs scared,
Autumn is noise,
From the local stadium,
Autumn is darkness,
Making things frightened,
Autumn is family,
In front of the fire,
Autumn is cold men,
Walking their dogs,
Autumn is cosy,
People together,
Autumn is cars,
With busy roads,
Autumn is fireworks,
Screeching and banging,
Autumn is mist,
Hard to see through.

James Sexton (11)
Wootton Bassett School

Christmas

C hristmas time has come once again,
H ibernate all the little creatures out there
R est little Lord Jesus,
I n the crib, tucked asleep as you lay.
S anta delivers the presents to all,
T ill the shine of the sun at day.
M erry Christmas to all, as you sleep
A nd a happy new year again.
S anta has gone once more, so take your stockings down
            and wait for next year!

Amy Aitken (11)
Wootton Bassett School

You

Your colours flare
As you soar into the air
On rainbow wings
Magical things.

This is your dream
Your own endless stream
Of thoughts unwind
From your beautiful mind.

Your dreams and ideas
Spreading like happy tears
Filling your brain
Like welcome rain.

Do anything, be anyone
Let your heart come undone
This is you! Say it loud
For what you are you should be proud.

True beauty lies within
Remember this when hope grows thin
When all faith has deserted you
Look inside and you'll see you.

Maddie Humphries (12)
Wootton Bassett School

The School Day

It begins with a class get-together,
Our tutor is at the end of her tether,
Followed by a lesson of French,
Trying to say branché but actually saying bench.
Then we're all off to period two,
After a quick visit to the loo.
Then we have a break,
Where we try to escape.
We are back in the classroom,
For a lesson of doom.
Off we go to our maths detention,
Instead of our delicious luncheon.
Now it's woodwork,
We've all gone berserk.
We get changed for PE,
We are forced to do cross-country.
We sit through a lesson of history,
But what we learnt is a mystery.
The day is over,
It's like finding a four-leafed clover.
We go home filled with sorrow,
Because we have to return tomorrow!

Sophie Warlow (12)
Wootton Bassett School

Autumn

Autumn reminds one
of itchy jumpers,
colourful and holey,
brought out
from underneath beds.

Autumn reminds one
of hot cocoa
and tasty crumpets,
though the butter
has long gone.

Autumn reminds one
of crackling fires,
sitting in front,
laughing happily,
snuggled up in a blanket.

Autumn reminds one
of the wind groaning
as it darts
from tree to tree,
rattling at windowpanes.

Sam Davies (11)
Wootton Bassett School